TRUE FIT

First published in 2014 by:
Graphera Publishing
Stockholm | Sweden

Office:
Olofsgatan 18
SE-111 36 Stockholm
info@graphera.se
www.grapherapublishing.com

First edition 2014

Hardcover ISBN 978-91-98-1375-1-4

Editor: Johanna Bjuhr Escalante
Translation: Ted Kurie
Photo: Fredrik Ottosson, www.fredrikottosson.se
Graphic design: Sarah Tjellander
Typographic illustration: Peter Liedberg/LetterBoy
Illustration: Terése Karlsson

Prepress: Repro360

Printed and bound by Gorenjski Tisk Storitve, Slovenia

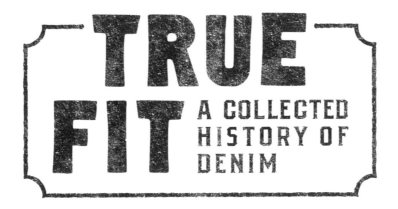

TRUE FIT
A COLLECTED HISTORY OF DENIM

VIKTOR FREDBÄCK

Photo: Fredrik Ottosson
Text: Rickard Eklund

Graphera
PUBLISHING

CONTENTS

I sat in my small, shabby student apartment during my studies at the university,
reading my roommate's magazines and books. The books were about vintage jeans, and my eyes
were instantly drawn to all the images. It was something that was missing in my student literature.
The stories told in those pages and through those garments immediately caught my interest.
It was like being able to experience an entire life's story through each blue garment.

The first and only vintage item I would buy – I thought back then – was a tiny doll dressed in jeans named Buddy Lee, made in the early 1920s. As a poor student, the purchase was hard on my wallet, but the fascination and curiosity I had for that Buddy Lee doll and the story surrounding it meant that I would soon be right back there, spending my rent money on something else I couldn't afford, this time a vintage garment.

I never thought that ten years later I would own the majority of the apparel I sat and stared at in those books, and would also create my own book on the subject. Largely for this I have to thank my mother, who passed away in 2012 – far too early. She always asked with a smile what I'd do with all my garments, which grew in number with each passing year. After her death, it became quite clear to me: I had to do something with my collection that had grown so large it was forcing me out of house and home. So the book you hold in your hands is dedicated to my mother, Maud Fredbäck.

For me, the hunt for vintage jeans has been so much more than merely filling holes in my collection. The thrill of the hunt – the adventure in itself – is a big part of the allure: everything from combing through five thousand hits on eBay every few days to searching in total darkness in old, abandoned mines from the 1800s. After a large dose of stubbornness and determination, finding what you are looking for is like being a kid at Christmas again.

Each garment reveals a peculiar history. To me, the story is not just about the garment manufacturers; it's also about each garment's unique owners. In some cases, I had been told stories about who originally wore the clothes I bought, stories which are also reflected throughout this book. The feeling of actually knowing the history of the person who wore the garment brings it back to life. And that makes it surprisingly easy to dream back to that time.

During my years as a traveling salesman in the fashion industry, I have all too often witnessed a garment's passing from the purchaser all the way to the end customer without any real knowledge of the garment itself being passed on. This sometimes results in facts being omitted or even made up. Thus, I have always had a desire to truly understand all of the garment's various details – why they are placed where they are, and why they look the way they do. But above all, I also want to understand the garment's original fit. It has been an intention of this book to be able to actually show these vintage garments' "True Fit".

Obviously, some information gets lost when the big brands of the past are up-ended by earthquakes and fires. And information collected from other sources is at times imprecise. I therefore find myself many times openly questioning whether the evidence is written in stone, or not.

I have been collecting jeans with the motto that it can never end, for if it did: what would be the point in collecting? I believe, however, that history is learned and worldviews expanded with every garment that is collected. To me, it's like putting together an enormous puzzle where knowledge grows with every piece put in place – but how the final image will look will forever remain unknown. The pieces have so far shaped this book: True Fit – A Collected History of Denim.

VIKTOR FREDBÄCK

IN THE GLOW
OF A HEADLAMP

*It's just turned dusk and the desert's starry sky is already
startlingly amazing. But where they're going there are no stars, only darkness.
After the four-hour drive from Las Vegas straight through the Nevada desert
followed by several hours of walking, they are finally in the right place.*

Viktor switches on the headlamp mounted to his helmet. A flash of light sweeps over the rocks to reveal a foot and a half tall black hole in front of his feet. Having unearthed this small opening, Mike has already disappeared into the tight void. A moment has passed since any noise could be heard from his snake-like crawl inside the earth. Now it's quiet. Mike's father-in-law Russ and friend Cory stand by, waiting their turn. Viktor squats down to look through the opening. It's dark, and he can't make out any light from Mike's headlamp.

"Mike?"

But there's no answer.

Viktor carefully squeezes himself into the old, derelict mine. It's so cramped inside that he has to turn his head to the side so that his helmet and headlamp don't get stuck. He shuffles forward, fearfully knowing he's beyond the point of no return. The surrounding stone coldly grasps him from all sides. If anything were to happen, he would have to navigate this inner passage

in order to slip out the other side. Viktor slithers on, using his elbows, and wedges forward with his toes. Down here the ground is cool and dry, and there is a fine layer of stone dust everywhere. He dispenses any feelings of claustrophobia as best he can and shines his light ahead.

He finally emerges out of the far end of the narrow passage and finds enough room to stand upright. Mike is there, smiling and illuminating him with his lamp. They stand in a mineshaft. The thick beams hold up the subterranean ceiling, but every so often stones have broken through, building rubble piles of various sizes on the mine's floor. Rails are fixed on the ground. Once used by miners to ferry carts in and out of the mountain, they are now almost completely hidden by stones, gravel and the quarter inch thick sheet of dust that covers everything in sight. With the slightest movement, this fine powder swirls up around their shoes to dance in the light of their lamps. They inhale filtered air through their breathing masks.

Then Viktor and Mike hear the next man coming in through the passage.

After a short while, everyone has gathered together and they continue deeper into the darkness of the mine. Their headlamps chase long shadows before them. Mike, one of the most experienced of the team, takes the lead. Starting in 1987, Mike began to accompany his father-in-law Russ on desert excursions, or as they call it, "bottle hunting". He and Russ would dig in the desert for old whiskey bottles, which they cashed in for a nice profit. But truth be told, Russ is the true veteran in the expedition party. He's been chasing bottles since 1967. It wasn't until years later that he and Mike started hunting for denim garments.

During one of their bottle hunts in 1988, Mike trampled over an entire vintage denim jacket, resulting in its destruction and infuriating him in the process. In a moment of epiphany, Mike realized that someday he might be able to uncover similar garments. In 1996, he found a pair of jeans. From that day forward he gave up bottle hunting and began searching exclusively for clothing.

Since then it's been a long learning process. In the beginning, neither Mike nor Russ knew anything about jeans, but they learned over time. They also learned how to read the terrain and find old mineshafts. They got to know that where there's one hole, there's more. But the search can be difficult; after all, these treasures are often buried under mountains of nondescript rubble. Some mines have been cordoned off with fences by order of the state, but most of them have already been plundered and therefore are not of much interest. In order to locate undiscovered mines, much of Mike and Russ's energy is spent hiking up and down the mountains, test digging for holes leading to mines. Sometimes it's like finding a needle in a haystack, and they must dig in several different places before hitting pay dirt.

These days, Mike and Russ do two to three expeditions per month.

Viktor's first contact with Mike was through eBay. He had been thinking about buying an antique pair of jeans for a long time and turned his quest to the net. Eventually he found Mike, who had become one of the world's leading jeans experts. Mike invited Viktor to the U.S. to search the desert mines together with him and Russ. It's been seven years since.

But the first time Viktor traveled to the States, he was filled with an uneasy sense of uncertainty, not knowing what lie ahead. However, this uncertainty quickly vanished as soon as he met Mike. And through the years they've gotten to know each other very well, becoming good friends.

Today, Viktor is the proud owner of a pair of jeans well over one hundred years old; one of the rarest relics of its kind. He can also rightly be considered one of the premier denim collectors in the world. Not that he owns the largest collection ever assembled; he does not. But because he might just have the most unique.

They continue through the mineshaft and stumble upon a room-sized space dug in the mountain where the shaft's walls widen. A pair of support beams has broken on one side, allowing the mountain wall to collapse inwards. The men begin their search in different places. Mike squats in front of a small hill of stones and begins sorting through it while Viktor finds a pile of trash worth rummaging. He kicks up the thin layer of stone dust while working. His headlamp scans the pile. He removes a handful of trash and sees something.

It's a fragment from an old newspaper.

He picks it up and reads. It's from the 1890s.

Newspapers are good indicators of the mine's age and when it was active. It is also one of the methods they use to date the jeans or cloth fragments they find, providing a rough indication of the garment's age.

Viktor describes it as a jigsaw puzzle. For every article of clothing he finds, the closer he comes to completing its puzzle with history. The adventure is tedious and time consuming as the team discovers an average of two complete garments a year. It's essential they take pleasure in the search itself in order to keep going. If Viktor had his druthers, the hunting and gathering would go on forever. Sometimes he's lucky enough to find something. Sometimes, however, it's simply not his day; it's someone else's. And today's just such a day.

While Viktor puts aside the magazine pages and delves further into the miners' old pile of junk, Mike calls out. His voice sounds muffled and different through the breathing mask:

"Check this out. I found something!"

△ CHARLA HARRIS, MARRIED TO MIKE. Works as a landscape architect in Los Angeles. She compiled Mike's book "Jeans of the Old West: A History". But Charla has also written her own book: "American Overalls". Originally, it was her father, Russ, who introduced her and Mike to "bottle hunting" and indirectly to vintage jeans. With good reason, one can most probably say that Charla's interest for the old and authentic is genetic. It remains to be seen if any of this has been inherited by her and Mike's two daughters, Lauren and Rachel.

◁ MICHAEL ALLEN HARRIS, AUTHOR OF THE BOOK "JEANS OF THE OLD WEST: A HISTORY". Mike works as a painter in California where he lives with his wife, Charla. Ever since 1987, Mike followed his father-in-law Russ on "bottle hunts" in the desert. But in 1996, he found an old pair of jeans during one of their expeditions. The rest is history. Today, Mike is considered to be one of the world's foremost experts on vintage jeans from the 1800s. It's probably also the reason why he takes it upon himself to find the appropriate nicknames for his friends. With tongue-in-cheek, he calls Victor, "Young 'Prentice".

△ CORY PIEHOWICZ WORKS AS A PHOTOGRAPHER in his hometown of Granville, Ohio. His biggest interest is collecting old photos and owns several thousand images from days gone by.

Cory met Michael Allen Harris on a web forum and subsequently joined him on one of his desert raids for jeans. They had done no more than dig down into their first mine when Cory found a pair of Levi's N° 2 from the late 1800s and was instantly hooked. Since then he has continued his search for old denim clothing.

His interest in history has led him to plan to publish a book about his vintage photo collection.

△ BOTTLE FROM THE 1800s.
Probably a beer bottle. It was found
in the desert in a "bottle hunt".

DREAMS OF GOLD AND SILVER

Mike holds up the jeans. In the glow of the light they see a small, rusty-red dust cloud dissipate into the air. The pants are contorted and closely resemble something like a thick, underground root. They straighten out with some difficulty, like an old man stretching his rheumatic legs.

Viktor, Russ and Cory gather around Mike. They begin to examine the crumpled jeans as the dust particles settle on the ground.

The pants are certainly well worn, like most garments of the day. The indigo color is faded out on the front thighs, and there are white specks from melted candle wax. Both legs have large holes at the knees. The left leg is cut off at the knee, and the right leg is missing a large piece of fabric from just below the knee to halfway down the shin.

There is a button fly – a standard for pants from this era. The ubiquitous zipper didn't appear until the late 1950s.

The backside of the jeans has a large hole in the right leg, while the left leg is completely missing. The remaining vestiges of denim are threadbare, providing anyone who would wear them with only partial covering, especially on their bottom. Not surprisingly, the denim is considerably worn out on the backside.

But there are more interesting details.

The pockets on the front have a wave-shaped double seam under the edges, a so-called *arcuate stitch*. A similar arcuate stitch is found on the small pocketwatch pocket. While the arcuate stitches provided no function, they are strikingly decorative.

The specimen Mike has discovered bears the mark of Meyerstein & Lowenberg, a San Francisco denim manufacturer owned by Prussian immigrants Lewis Meyerstein and Isidor Lowenberg.

Isidor came to America in 1853 and Lewis immigrated around the same time. They both married wives from Alabama who were born to Prussian and Bavarian parents. In 1861, Isidor and Lewis opened the doors to their first business in San Francisco – a clothing distribution company. It wasn't until 1877 that they began producing clothing themselves. Two years later, Isidor was awarded a patent for an improvement in work apparel, and the company began to produce jeans under the patent in 1880.

The Meyerstein & Lowenberg partnership continued until 1887, after which Isidor opened a business with his son, aptly named Lowenberg & Company. Lewis Meyerstein continued to make clothes under his own name and was eventually joined by his son in 1894. Separately, these two companies manufactured work clothing under the name *Pacific Coast*, probably using Isidor's patent from 1879.

The most interesting thing about Mike's newfound jeans is the detail on the sides of the pockets where arrowhead-shaped stitches are found. Called a *dart stitch*, this method was used as one of many solutions to reinforce pockets during the era.

It's a clear indication the jeans are made sometime before the year 1890.

They continue deeper into the mine. The sound of their shoes on the mine floor echoes back at them, almost creating the eerie feeling they're being followed. Their visibility reaches no farther than the lights of the headlamps. Everything else is dark.

The light tells the tale of the shaft, pointing out each protruding edge and corner as they walk through. From a distance, smooth surfaces appear as if they are coated with oil in the headlamps' glow, creating an ever-changing mosaic of shadows.

Viktor is last in line with Mike in front of him. While they walk, Mike gently folds the jeans he has found. Russ and Cory have moved ahead, and their black silhouettes can be seen further down the shaft. Mike and Viktor increase their speed in order to catch up. As the foursome charges ahead through the mine, darkness closes like a curtain behind them.

Mike's newly discovered jeans, or *waist overalls* as they were originally called, were worn in the late 1800s by a miner who must have toiled day in and day out down in the shaft. Of course, the modern protections enjoyed by miners today didn't exist back then. There were no helmets or breathing masks to filter out stone dust and heavy metal particulates that permeated the air. The miner of the 19th century had only his denim jeans for protection.

It was extremely hard work in rough conditions. The lives of gold and silver mine workers were quite difficult and dangerous. A gold digger would first dig up a foot or two of topsoil. He would then put a shovel of dirt in his miner's pan and take it to a nearby stream or river to begin panning the dirt, sand, gravel and larger stones in the water. This process continued over and over again until only gold and other heavy minerals

remained. If the gold digger was lucky, he might end up with one to five dollars worth of metal in his pan. This was a time consuming method, and it often took a whole day to collect just two teaspoons of gold.

On average, a miner earned between three and twelve dollars a day. Perhaps this seems like a lot of money for the era, but one has to take into account a miner's startup costs, which easily added up to seven hundred fifty dollars just to equip himself and go into business. He needed a tent and something to sleep in, various camping equipment to cook food, tarpaulins and, of course, clothes. Beyond the basic necessities, the miner also needed tools such as shovels, picks, crowbars and sledgehammers. Moreover, it was often critical to carry cholera tablets because disease easily spread in the unhygienic living and working conditions inhabited by the miners.

Despite their best-intentioned preparations, many succumbed to the harsh lifestyle. It wasn't only an adverse environment of climate and weather, threats of disease and the backbreaking work itself – there was also the danger of other people nearby. If a miner found success, he could be sure that it would upset someone.

Many miners were robbed and beaten to death. Not only was their gold stolen, but also their supplies, which were difficult to obtain in the desert.

In fact, it's estimated that between 1848, the year when the California Gold Rush started, and 1855, a total of three hundred seventy million dollars worth of gold was mined, or about forty-six million dollars worth per year. Yet, most prospectors leaving their former farm and city occupations to take up work in the mine were not greeted with riches. An average miner panned to career earnings of roughly seven hundred fifty dollars – the amount he originally spent in supplies to begin mining.

In other words, it was a bust for most people. One historian has claimed that ninety-nine percent of all miners would have been better off financially if they had not left their previous occupations.

But gold fever was a dream that meant a better life for the prospector and his family.

It was a chance to rise above life's trials and tribulations.

And it was difficult to argue against the benefits of a gold rush experienced by those who succeeded in being a part of it.

In order to protect themselves against injury, weather, the night's cold and the day's scorching sun, and numerous other threats, miners depended on their denim garments. No other fabric of the day was up to par.

In the late 1800s, jeans were the mandatory

uniform of the miner. If men worked for a mining company, they were loaned workers clothing. Since the jeans were owned by the mining companies, workers had to put on their denims when entering the mine and return the denims upon exiting. This was probably in part a security measure to aid worker safety, but it also mitigated worker theft of precious metals. By forcing workers to undress after their shifts, they could easily be monitored to ensure they didn't walk away with what really belonged to the mine owners. Another reason may have been to do with the mining companies' inability to wash jeans on site. Because it was too expensive to do in the U.S., the garments were shipped back and forth to China to be washed. Incredibly, this outsourced method proved to be cheaper.

But one day the unthinkable happened.

The gold dried up in California as early as the mid-1850s.

It was a financial disaster for miners who had not struck it rich. These unfortunate souls would have to find other means to support themselves, maybe by going back to the farms they neglected for years or begging to get their old jobs back, which was not a very likely outcome. All hope seemed to have disappeared.

But very soon news spread like wildfire around the country.

Someone had found silver in the Nevada desert. Lots of silver.

And that's when the fever came rushing back again – albeit silver fever this time. People from far and wide quickly traveled to Nevada to lay claim to their own little slice of wealth and success.

The gold rush was just one of many events that took place during the second half of the 1800s. It was a turbulent time in California and the United States at large. There was a lot happening and many technological advances were made. Beyond the U.S. horizon, several wars were taking place in various parts of the world.

Fresh in memory was the Mexican-American War, where the U.S. took over land previously belonging to Mexico. This included California.

The American Civil War also took place during this time, as well as the Indian Wars. Despite the turmoil, one significant achievement was the abolition of slavery in the U.S.

In the 1880s, violent pogroms were carried out against Jews in Russia after a rumor erupted that Jews were behind the assassination of Tsar Alexander II. Thousands of Jewish homes were destroyed and a violent campaign swept over large parts of the country. Many Russian Jews fled to America to escape persecution.

But they were far from the only ones heading to America at this time. During the century's last two decades, around ten million Europeans immigrated to America. In their original countries, times were very hard for emigrants and many had lived on the breadline. They traveled with the hope that they could make a better life in the U.S., but everyday life would prove to be difficult for most of them – even on the other side of the Atlantic.

Still, the second half of the 1800s was not categorized only by war and misery.

Perhaps one of the most important events and technological innovations that characterized the late 1800s was experimentation with aerial vehicles in several parts of the world, efforts that predate the Wright brothers' first officially recognized flight in 1903. But just as man was taking to the air, he was also traveling farther down into the earth.

Mike, Viktor, Russ and Cory continue exploring the mine and arrive at one of the many wooden doors mounted in the shafts. The door is completely dilapidated and looks like it will fall apart at any moment.

The miners used to sector-off different shafts with doors to minimize any draft passing through. Without these doors, air could blow so hard that it would extinguish the miners' candles. In order to prevent the wind gusts from coming through the gaps in the door boards, the miners sealed the cracks with pieces of jeans from garments they could no longer use. Viktor and Mike's crew often encounter such makeshift work. The use of jeans as sealants in the mines is one of the reasons that they find many disassembled pants missing, for example, a leg here or there.

The team enters through the door and arrives at a fork. One of the shafts is cut off by a landslide, but the other continues downward. Steps are carved into the stone.

A little later they are in a larger room surrounded by piles of rock and debris.

Viktor, Cory and Russ search in the glow of their headlamps, the sound of their digging bounces between the stone walls. A short distance away, Mike examines his old vintage jeans.

The history of denim begins much earlier than the time of the Gold Rush and far from both California and the Nevada desert.

In the southeastern French town of Nimes, a twill

fabric, originally made from silk and called *serge de Nîmes*, was manufactured for many years. True to its origin, the word *serge* comes from the Latin *sericus*, meaning silk.

Cotton was later mixed in with the *serge de Nîmes* and woven with blue weft and white warp. Hence the reason why old, used jeans become lighter, sometimes even white in places – the indigo-dyed weft becomes broken down or pale.

This fabric became known as denim in America as early as 1695.

The word *jeans* originally comes from the French name for the Italian city of Genoa, where they made garments of cloth – hardly the same quality as traditional denim. The word did not enter the common vernacular until the 1930s. They were previously called waist overalls.

With one thumb, Mike rubs lightly on an arrowhead stitch near a pocket and points his light at it. These jeans were made during a time when Levi Strauss & Co. still held the patent for riveted pockets.

The idea that a small detail such as a copper rivet could hold such importance in the history of jeans is truly amazing.

△ THIS PHOTO WAS TAKEN sometime in the 1880s. The man's waist overalls are most likely a pair of Levi's. This can be determined by looking at the riveted pockets. During this period, Levi Strauss & Company's patent for riveted pockets was still in active, and the company sued anyone who tried to imitate them or infringe on their patent.

△ A COMMON SOLUTION USED DOWN IN THE SILVER MINES was to fasten a candle to a hat, thus functioning as a kind of contemporary headlamp.

MEYERSTEIN & LOWENBERG
PACIFIC COAST 1886

△ SEVERAL BRANDS USED SO-CALLED *DART STITCH* between 1873 and 1890. Neustadter Brothers used them on their Boss of the Road jeans; Levi Strauss & Co. on its Grizzly clothing, as manufactured from the late 1870s to early 1880s. A.B. Elfelt & Company, Pioneer Overalls and a brand from Montana, which unfortunately disappeared from history, also used the dart stitch.

△ THE SMALL DIMPLE IN THE METAL indicates that the rivet is most likely manufactured in a factory, not by a "piece worker".

THE WEAK LINK

There was a big problem with early jeans. Jacob Davis, a Latvian tailor from Riga, knew this all too well. He would eventually revolutionize jeans and partner with one of the industry's most prominent figureheads. However, only one of them would become a household name – and it wasn't Davis.

Jacob Davis immigrated to America sometime in the mid-1800s. He immediately began tailoring in his new homeland in a variety of places, albeit without much success. He also tried his hand at gold mining and brewing, but again, without attaining any real career breakthrough.

Following the California Gold Rush and the discovery of the large silver deposit in the Nevada desert in the 1850s, Jacob settled in Reno and began sewing work clothing.

Jacob often received requests from miners to mend their pants, but didn't give it a second thought until a woman came into his shop one day and ordered a pair of work pants for her husband. She was frustrated and told Jacob that her husband's trousers always suffered tears, especially at the pockets. She stared intensely at Jacob and demanded that the new jeans he provided would last. Davis quickly realized that the woman's complaint was a very common problem for most workers, and that many of his customers experienced the same issue. The jeans of the day were simply not tough enough and the weak link was the pockets.

The work that miners performed inflicted ma-jor wear and tear on their garments. Miners crawled around on their hands and knees underground, worked kneeling down, and probably used their pockets to carry both tools and stones.

Davis knew he had to do something.

He got a simple yet revolutionary idea when he examined the various saddle blankets he sewed, which were reinforced with copper rivets along the edges. Davis took this concept and applied it to his jeans – reinforcing the sides of the pockets with rivets. Shortly thereafter, the woman returned, picked up the garment for her husband and left the shop.

Davis had no idea that he caught lightning in a bottle that day.

In little time, the rumor of his durable, long-lasting pants spread among the miners and he soon found himself with more work than he could handle. Miners were keen to acquire a pair of rivet-reinforced pants, or at the very least, wanted him to retrofit their current garments with rivets.

Due to diehard competition, Davis realized he had to protect his idea, but at the same time he knew he could not afford the legal costs. So he wrote a letter to his denim dealer in San Francisco and asked for help with a patent, sending it via certified mail to Levi Strauss.

Levi Strauss had a significant amount of business experience. Upon arriving in New York from Germany at age eighteen, he was given the opportunity to sharpen his business skills at a company owned by his two older brothers. They owned a grocery store in town and allowed Levi to work there for a while. Young Levi soon took to the road and earned his living as a traveling salesman, or *peddler*, as they were called back then. It was a normal job, especially for Jews who had immigrated. The job provided a great way for immigrants to learn English and become Americans. Levi did it for a few years before coming up with the idea to open a branch of his brothers' New York-based company in San Francisco.

This was at a time before railways stretched all the way to California. Levi traveled first in a steamer, which was a smaller type of vessel, along the Gulf of Mexico coast to Panama. Many ships traveled to Panama and Nicaragua because the two countries had the narrowest land crossings between the Atlantic and Pacific.

In Panama, Levi and his fellow passengers debarked the ship and started their journey up the Chagres River. After that, they hiked on foot all the way to Panama City, carrying their belongings the entire route. When they reached the Pacific Ocean, Levi and the others jumped on board another steamer that took them all the way north to San Francisco.

When Levi reached San Francisco, he almost immediately sold all the goods he had brought with him. He was only twenty-four years old at the time. One miner told Levi that it was a shame he didn't have any pants with him, as they were in short supply among prospectors panning for gold in the mountains.

This made Levi ponder.

He took the brown canvas he had brought with him through his arduous journey and visited a tailor to have a pair of pants fashioned. Sure enough, a miner bought the pants straight away.

A short while after he came to San Francisco, Levi purchased a business license from the city and opened a small grocery store with his brother-in-law, David Stern. Their business was located near the harbor, which was a center of activity in the city at the time. San Francisco was still relatively isolated in the 1850s and depended heavily on goods brought in by ship. The port was therefore a vibrant place full of workers, pubs, and shops. In 1853, there were as many as twenty-three loading docks with bustling dockworkers loa-

ding and unloading goods, and traders buying and selling them. It was imperative for vendors to get to incoming ships quickly because arriving too late or losing bids to competitors typically resulted in failure. As such, trading in the harbor meant either a full month's income or an entire month's loss. If vendors took a loss, they had to wait out the month until the next ship arrived. Ships sometimes wrecked off of Tierra del Fuego while en route to San Francisco. It took even longer for the next shipment to arrive when this happened. In other words, the supply of goods was erratic at best.

Many merchants hired young boys to stand watch and keep an eye on the horizon outside the harbor in order to alert the merchants when a ship arrived. These lookouts increased the merchants' chances of getting the first-pick of goods and filling their stockrooms.

In the beginning, Levi and David Stern dealt exclusively with groceries. Eventually though, they began providing for the needs of gold prospectors and their families. At this time of business expansion, Levi and Stern had no in-house production of waist overalls and opted to subcontract out work to freelance tailors. Denim was the fabric of choice, but sometimes it was hard to come by. When denim was in short supply, pants were made out of canvas, or *duck*, as it was called.

As the years passed, Levi built up a good reputation among a customer base that included tailors, shop owners in small communities and workers. He became known as honest and reliable.

When Levi received the letter from Jacob Davis, he knew who it was because of their solid business relationship. Levi and Davis had done a lot of commerce together over the years.

Levi immediately understood the value of Davis's rivet innovation and wrote back that he agreed to pay the sixty-eight dollars for the cost of the patent. He felt it could be a perfect chance for his company to expand.

Viktor, Russ, and Cory continue searching with their headlamps. Mike gently folds the jeans he's found and places them in his backpack. It's been a good day for him. A really good day.

The waist overalls Mike has discovered are from 1886. They calculated this year based on the pant's design and the newspaper fragments found in the shaft.

The crew continues their search deeper into the mine. The sound of their shoes crunching over gravel and stone echoes through the cavern. Timber support beams pass by at irregular intervals in the glow of the light.

Suddenly Mike stops and holds up his hand.

"What is it?" Viktor asks.

Mike silently motions with a nod at the dense darkness a yard in front of his feet.

There is a shaft.

It's a pitch-black chasm in the rock, a narrow gap of darkness.

But it's no more than a yard and a half to the other side. They ponder jumping the abyss and continuing on their way, but Mike has a feeling that there might be something at the bottom of the shaft. He just wants to know how deep it is before he decides to climb down.

They remove a fifty-yard length of rope from a backpack.

Mike ties a big knot on one end and bends over the edge, carefully feeding more and more rope down into the abyss. Viktor stands behind him with the rope reel in his arms and dispenses one arm length at a time.

After a while, Viktor has unraveled all the rope from his arms.

He pats Mike on the back and tells him there's no more line to feed down the shaft.

They lie down with their heads on the edge and shine their headlamps down into the darkness.

They can clearly see the beginning of the rope in the glow of light near the surface, but darkness swallows the rope as it stretches farther down. The rope hangs like a plumb straight down into dark water, slowly swaying and stirring small ripples.

Viktor and Mike glance at each other before they try to see the end of the rope.

Suddenly, they can see it.

Jacob Davis quickly moved to San Francisco to start work as a master tailor and foreman at Levi Strauss & Co.'s newly opened factory where production of rivet-reinforced work wear was underway. When Levi's initially opened their jeans factory in 1873, the company subcontracted tailors to manufacture the jeans. These freelancers worked from their homes in California or New York.

A detail worth noting is that it's possible to distinguish the difference between Levi's factory-made jeans and those made by outside tailors by inspecting the rivets. The factory had a special machine that hammered in the rivets. This left a distinct imprint on the metal. The freelance tailors often could not afford such a machine and ended up doing the work by hand.

In the 1870s, unemployment among whites was very high and Strauss, who was well aware of residents' concerns that his new factory would only employ Chinese, surprised everyone. Instead of Chinese personnel, as many competitors used, Levi's chose to hire only whites. Strauss even used it in the company's marketing, selling his waist overalls with the slogan: "White Labor Only."

Levi's continued to use "white labor" in its advertising for the rest of the 1800s. But there remains a question as to the accuracy of this policy as it is common knowledge that Levi's fabric cutter was Chinese. Many whites attempted the difficult job of cutting fabric, but only the Chinese worker managed it with success. As such, he remained with the company. Also, it is still uncertain if there were more non-white workers at Levi's.

As early as June 2, 1873, weeks after the patent was approved, Levi's sold their first pair of jeans with rivet-reinforced pockets.

In just one year, Levi's sold twenty-one thousand six hundred pairs of pants and jackets with riveted pockets made of denim or duck. Their clothing was very popular with miners, cowboys, lumberjacks, and other rugged professionals. The rumor was out that Levi's work wear was the best quality and that it wore very well.

There were a hundred different jean manufacturers in the second half of the 1800s, but Levi's had quality – no one could take that away from them. Although their riveted waist overalls were often more expensive than most other brands, Levi's far outsold the competition.

The superior sales at Levi's may have been the reason they developed a new, cheaper model of jeans made from lesser quality denim. Nonetheless, these more affordable jeans sold well. The new model became known as N° 2 and was produced from the late 1880s to the end of the 1930s. But Levi's original jeans were called XX – and became the inspiration for the famous Levi's 501 jeans model.

The XX was made of nine ounces of Amoskeag Blue Denim, which was the best quality product from the best denim producer in the country. Many companies bought their fabric from Amoskeag, whether they were big brands or freelance entrepreneurs.

The N° 2 model was also made with nine ounces of Blue Denim, but the fabric was from an unspecified origin. N° 2's also had the same weight as the XX model, but with a little less quality. In addition, they used cotton thread for stitching seams and not the more expensive and durable linen thread used in XX seams.

Davis's invention of riveted pockets would not be the only way in which he changed the history of jeans. After Davis moved to California, he developed the design for which Levi's would become renowned.

Basically all jeans at this time had a *cinch strap* on the rear and only one back pocket. Jean jackets, or *blouses* as they were called back then, also had only one pocket. Davis, who was accustomed to sewing suits and smart trousers, borrowed a design element from more formal clothing. He put an extra back pocket on his trousers and an extra pocket on his jean jackets so that there was one on each side of the button-down opening.

Soon, many other jeans companies started to emulate Levi's design.

Since Levi's owned the patent on the rivets from 1873 to 1890, all other jean companies had to come up with their own solutions to enhance their pockets. But some disingenuously tried to capitalize on Levi's idea. A.B. Elfelt & Company was one such outfit that tried to market a copy of Levi's riveted pockets, but Levi's sued them in response. This lawsuit sent a clear message to all others to develop their own inventions instead of copying or stealing.

During the four years following 1873, nine patents were issued - each with a separate way to reinforce the pockets of waist overalls. Another six patents were granted in 1881.

Some companies used arrowhead seams, also called *dart stitch*, such as Meyerstein & Lowenberg. S. R. Krouse sewed partial pieces of fabric on top of the sides of pockets for reinforcement. B. & O. Greenebaum Company had reinforcing material that ran down over the pocket corner to a triangular shape and continued in a crescent all the way above the pocket opening. Chuang Quan Wo, a Chinese man who worked for Heynemann & Company, had a patent for small, strengthening leather pieces sewn on top of the pockets' corners.

There was no end to the variations.

In 1886, Levi's began placing a leather label on the back of their waist overalls. Clearly imprinted on the labels was an illustration of two horses vainly trying to pull apart a pair of Levi's pants. This became known as the *pulling label* and clearly denoted that this was a pair of authentic Levi's rivet-reinforced jeans.

However, Levi's was not the first to use this type of label. Banner Bros. Company started using a pulling label as early as 1878, meaning Strauss either copied the mark or, at the very least, let himself be inspired by it when designing his own mark with the two horses. Either way, this was one of the earliest examples of what we now refer to as *brand identity*.

Levi's XX model had a leather patch with the company name imprinted at the top. Underneath the logo was the image of the horses. The words *Copper Riveted Clothing* were written under the illustration.

Levi's Nº 2's used a patch of cloth instead of leather. It had exactly the same layout and design as the XX, but with a small change in phrasing: *Patent Riveted Clothing*.

The question is whether XX also had the word *Patent* on their labels. Because the marks were made with leather, they have since dried and aged to such a degree that they are completely unreadable today. On the other hand, the clarity of the illustration and text on Nº 2 labels still remains after all these years.

Many wanted to emulate this newfound idea of business branding. In 1887, Harrison & H. Company marketed a badge depicting two dogs trying to tear apart a pair of one of their jeans. This came only a year after Levi's released their brand image portraying the horses.

The Boss, a company based in Los Angeles, had a mark of two elephants trying to tear apart a pair of pants.

Competition between companies was shameless.

In many cases, jeans went without labeling, especially when made by small business owners who purchased their denim from the Amoskeag Mill. The weight of the fabric and its origin, not the brand, were the deciding factors for many vendors and their customers.

Most brands of yesteryear have long since disappeared due to various economic setbacks. But a company that launched a fresh, new idea had the potential to become an overnight success.

They see the knot in the rope.

It's far, far down there.

It dangles along the rock wall nearly a hundred fifty feet down in the depths, but the rope has not hit bottom. Beyond the rope's knot is nothing but total blackness.

Viktor pulls up the rope, rolls it up and puts it back in the backpack. There's not much else that can be done but pack up and go.

Viktor ponders his theory of rivets in jeans while they walk back to the mine's entrance.

Jacob Davis certainly had no idea as to the impact they would have on jeans when he began using them to make work wear. His main goal was to address a recurring problem his customers experienced and to make them happy. In doing so, his simple idea proved to make jeans very popular among workers of the day. It was an innovation many of Levi's competitors began to copy immediately after their patent expired in 1890.

Without this rivet innovation, workers' jeans, or the denim phenomenon at large, may never have occurred.

J. W. DAVIS.
Fastening Pocket-Openings.

No. 139,121.

Patented May 20, 1873.

Fig. 1.

Witnesses

J. L. Borne

C. M. Richardson

Inventor

Jacob W. Davis

per Dewey & Co.

Attys

△ "TO ALL WHOM IT MAY CONCERN: BE IT KNOWN THAT I, JACOB W. DAVIS, OF RENO, COUNTY OF WASHOE AND STATE OF NEVADA HAVE INVENTED AN IMPROVEMENT IN FASTENING SEAMS…"

So begins Jacob Davis's patent application for riveted pockets. The document then follows with a detailed explanation of the invention. He writes that the trouser pocket often tears when the user places his hands into the pockets, which is a significant strain on the garment. To reinforce the pocket, Davis explains that he uses a rivet, an eyelet or other similar metal button. Then he describes how the process works, and the result it gives.

Further down in the application, Davis notes that he knows of an existing and similar patent, but it is for the reinforcing of seams in shoes with rivets. Davis declares that his invention does not copy this earlier patent and concludes by writing:

"IN WITNESS WHEREOF I HEREUNTO SET MY HAND AND SEAL." /Jacob W. Davis

CHUANG QUAN WO 1874

There have been small triangular pieces of leather fastened to the pocket corners of these pants, but because they were made of leather, they have long since disintegrated.

Chuang Quan Wo was the name of the man behind the patent in question. He must have been one of Heynemann & Company's most inventive employees. He probably was granted far more patents than just this one.

Wo's jeans are made with two-by-one twill, also called uneven weave or "warp-face twill". Two-by-one is called uneven weave because it is more warp than weft on the surface. In layman's terms, it means there are more colored threads on the surface than white ones. The white threads are weaved in underneath. Two-by-one is a strong and durable fabric, making it ideal to produce denim with.

Another interesting detail that is typical of the time: the buttonholes in the fly are hand sewn, revealing that the pants were made sometime before the year 1880 – before the buttonhole machine was invented and patented.

Just like Wo's patent, these pants come from a truly early period in jeans history: 1874.

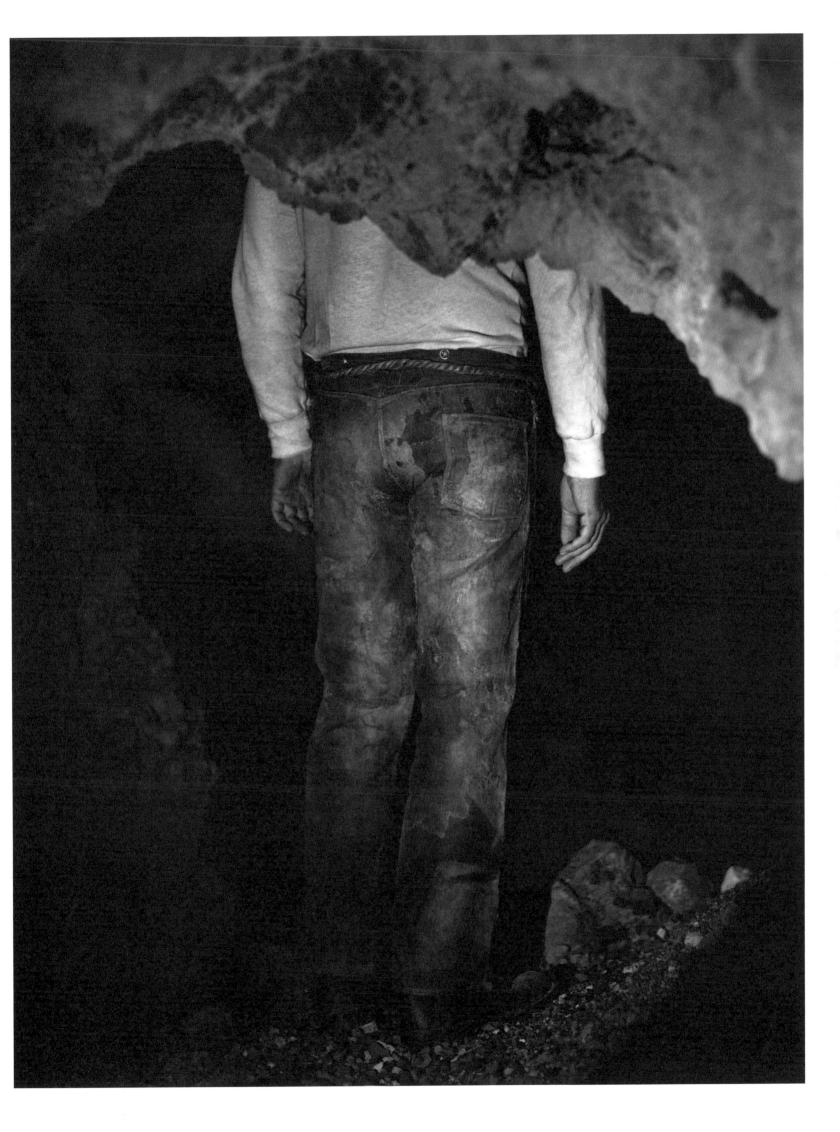

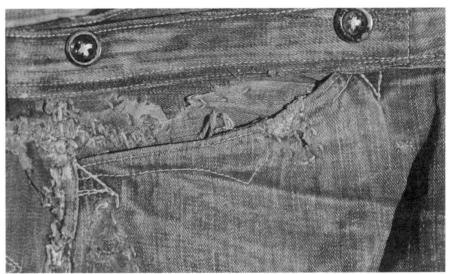

MINER'S HAT

A miner's hat, complete with wax droppings from candles. Candles were,
for a long time, the only source of illumination available down in the mines until
the early 1890s, when the newly invented carbide lamp replaced them.

LEVI'S №2 1901—10

Between 1886 and 1912–1913, Levi's made five small changes in their pulling label – the one with the horses. The changes are so small and meticulous that they can easily be missed if one doesn't examine them with close detail – but that is precisely what Michael Allen Harris and his wife Charla have done.

Levi's changed, among other things, the angle of one of the horse's legs as well as the angle of the man's arm holding the whip. The question is: why did they make these small changes? Was it a desire to try to maximize sales, or was it purely for aesthetic reasons?

The patch on these Levi's № 2's from 1901 to 1910 reveals that they belong to the fourth generation of the changes.

THE YEAR WAS 1891 when this newspaper advertisement was published. A year before that, Levi Strauss & Company's patent for rivets ran out, so anyone was free to capitalize on their invention. Maybe this was one of the reasons Levi's continued with their slogan "White Labor Only" – because it distinguished the company from the rest? Or perhaps it was an attempt to maintain its prominent position in the market?

These are most likely the oldest N° 2's in existence. The model is technically named *Levi's 201*, but came to be called N° 2's and were manufactured from 1888–1889 until 1941.

The N° 2 was the little brother of Levi Strauss & Company's flagship XX model and cheaper to produce for several obvious reasons. N° 2's were of a lesser quality – both the fabric and the threads in the seams were of a lower grade. Even the patch was made of cloth and not leather like the XX. So one may ask, when Levi's seemed to prioritize quality above all else, why were N° 2's ever launched in the first place?

Perhaps the answer lies in the fact that N° 2 pants went into production just before Levi's patent for riveted pockets ran out. Maybe they were worried about losing a large portion of their sales to other, less expensive denim brands. Because of the high price of their original XX jeans, could one argue their concern might be justified?

In any case, with the cheaper model N° 2's, Levi's could use its formidable strength to muscle into the market in a way that they could not before.

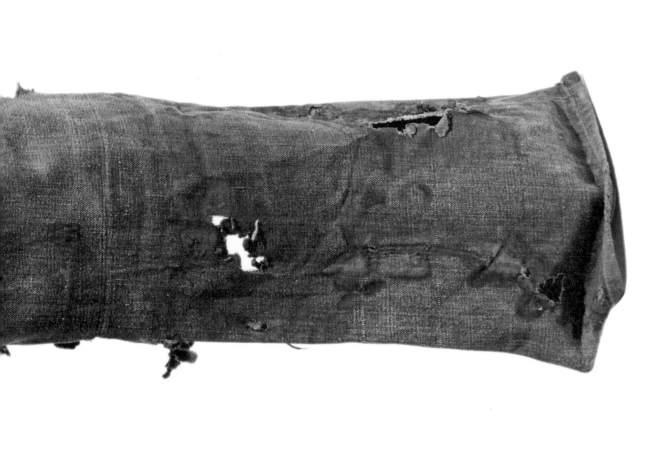

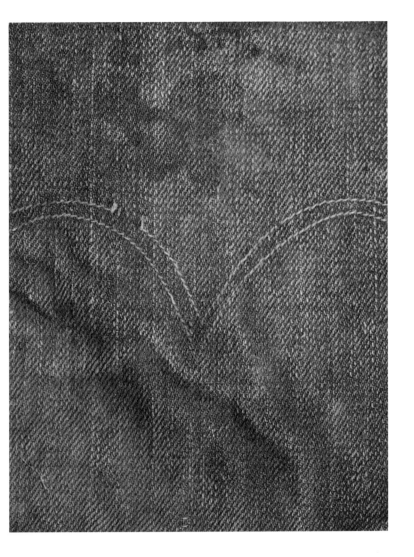

△ PULLING LABEL

THROUGH THE EYE OF A NEEDLE

*Viktor leans against the rock wall. It feels dry and cold against his hand.
He drags his fingertips along the wall while he follows the others back towards
the exit. His breath hisses through the filter of his breathing mask.*

They continue through the shaft, and Mike tells a story about when he and Charla visited a Nevada silver mine that was active in the 1940s and '50s. He remembers that the tunnel – a hundred yards in length – looked surprisingly modern. Further onward, the tunnel snaked left and right, unraveling a series of additional tunnels.

Two years later, Mike returned to this same mine with Russ. They came to an intersection and forked off to the right. When they exited the long tunnel, everything looked different. They found debris from the 1870s and '80s and realized they'd stepped back in time. On the other side of a pile of trash, Mike found a pair of vintage jeans and an old quilt from the same time period.

It turned out the mine was originally in use during the 1870s. It initially closed in the 1880s because only low-grade silver ore was found. The mine reopened in the 1940s when advances in extraction methods led to more profitable mining.

The mine they now walk through is also from the 1800s – and at least as old and dangerous.

They turn the bend and find a narrow opening in front of them. It is the exit.

During the 1920s, it was common for denim companies to use a *Union Ticket* – a little note sewn on the inside of jeans that guaranteed factory workers were adequately paid and worked in appropriate conditions. It was a simple way for many brands to show they had their workers' best interests in mind. However, not all manufacturers used them. Levi's waist overalls allegedly lacked union tickets because the company's stance was their staff already had good working conditions. In the late 1800s, Levi's marketed their jeans under the slogan "White Labor Only" as a way to capitalize on the fact that the company used local, white workers instead of Chinese, like many of their competitors did. After Levi Strauss died in 1902, his successors at Levi's continued running the company with the same goodwill.

Working conditions gradually improved in the late 1800s. It was around this time that the broader labor movement grew stronger. By 1866, the first trade union in the United States, the National Labor Union (NLU), was formed. Unfortunately, this union soon fell apart, but it left a legacy soon to be adopted by others.

The next union was formed just three years later and was comprised of seven hundred thousand members at its peak. Their primary focus was to stop child labor and pass eight-hour workday legislation.

Perhaps the most famous union, the American Federation of Labor (AFL), was founded in 1886 and had one million four hundred thousand members at its peak. The AFL successfully managed to raise wages for their members and increase safety in the workplace.

The emergence of trade unions would change working conditions for most companies – even jeans companies. But neither unions nor ethical business regulations were enough to mitigate the difficult economic environment that would come during the interwar period.

Likewise, the 1920s and '30s were a pretty dark period in the history of jeans.

It was largely due to a small insect named the *Boll Weevil*.

The boll weevil came from Mexico across the Rio Grande sometime in the 1890s. It is a small beetle, just less than a quarter of an inch long, with a trunk-like snout and a notorious appetite for cotton. It eats both cotton buds and flowers, and lays eggs inside the cotton itself – about two hundred at a time. Under optimal conditions, the species can reach eight to ten generations in a single cotton-growing season.

In the mid-1920s, the boll weevil beetle reached all cotton producing regions in the United States. It was the biggest destroyer of cotton crop in North America. Mississippi State University estimates that it has cost cotton producers roughly thirteen billion dollars since the beetle was first discovered in the U.S.

The boll weevil invasion was actually a major contributing factor to the Great Depression among cotton producers.

However, at least one positive thing came from the boll weevil beetle invasion: farmers realized that they were too dependent on cotton and started to grow other crops. This shift eventually contributed to economic diversification and greater biodiversity in the southern United States.

When the Great Depression came, the unions had no choice but to compromise on their demands so their members could continue to make a living and put food on the table.

Although the Great Depression started in September of 1929, it took off when the stock market crashed on what's known as *Black Tuesday* in October of the same year. Personal wages, tax revenues, corporate profits and prices plummeted as international trade declined by more than 50 percent.

But disaster had only just begun.

Unemployment soared. Around one in four people in the United States became unemployed, and in some other countries the number rose to one in three. Cities dependent on heavy industry were particularly hard-hit. Production virtually ceased in some countries.

Farmers and rural areas in the U.S. probably experienced the worst effects as crop prices fell by about 60 percent. In particular, cash crops, including cotton, were the heaviest hit. Many farmers were forced to give up their occupation because of falling prices, which contributed even more to the increasing unemployment. In turn, hundreds of small, local banks couldn't keep their doors open. One of the reasons farmers could no longer farm was partly due to the transition from more scalable small farming methods that used horses and mules, to larger scale, less flexible methods that relied on tractors and other motorized vehicles.

Viktor writhers through the mine's small exit hole and feels the cool night air pass over his face. He comes out, steps up and away from the mine and beats the dust and dirt off his clothing. Mike is already a few feet away and seems to be looking for something in his backpack.

Viktor takes off his helmet and breathing mask. The desert air is fresh and it's chilly out, colder here than inside the mine where the temperature is uniform. But Viktor thinks it's nice to breathe without a mask again. He sees Mike unscrew the cap of a water bottle and take a sip.

Soon, both Cory and Russ have exited. They brush themselves off as well, take off their mining equipment and also grab a drink of water.

The blackness of the heavens stretches over their heads. The moon is aglow and strong enough to cast shadows. In its vicinity, starlight fades, but everywhere else in the night sky the stars cast their ancient light, stretching across time and space.

Without wasting time, the team begins their trek back to the car. Mike goes first with his glowing headlamp still attached to his head as Cory, Russ, and Viktor follow closely behind. They are four illuminated shadows finding their way through the darkness.

The boll weevil – and the severe cotton shortage it

caused – meant tougher competition between jean manufacturers. Levi's chose to spend a fortune on advertising during this time to try to keep the company afloat. When the Great Depression began, Levi's – under its new leader Walter Haas – took measures to make the company profitable again. It guaranteed "a new pair of pants free if they rip". And if a pair of jeans was returned with a flaw, Levi's sought to learn from their mistake: they examined the jeans and corrected the manufacturing defect in the entire production line. Seemingly, the tradition of quality that Levi Strauss upheld during his life was still important to the company.

In 1931, twelve million Americans were without jobs and Levi Strauss & Co.'s sales had plummeted. In order to keep as many employees working as possible, the company decreased its number of working hours per week.

The company struggled throughout the '30s. Gradually, sales numbers started to increase and employees returned to full-time hours again.

Levi's flagship product at the time was their 501 jeans. The model had remained unchanged ever since Jacob Davis designed and patented the first pair. But that original design would soon see an overhaul.

The rivets on the back were covered over so as not to scratch furniture, car seats or saddles. After a camping trip, Walter Haas decided to remove the rivet under the fly at the front of the pants. He had been standing near a fireplace and noticed what all the cowboys already knew: this particular rivet quickly warmed up and eventually burned the wearer.

Small changes were therefore necessary.

In 1922, Levi's started using belt loops on its jeans, even though suspenders would remain the preferred method of holding up pants through the '30s. Overall buttons remained a part of the design until 1936 when they were removed for good. When it comes to belt loops, it's worth noting that Levi's was not the first to implement them. There were other companies using belt loops as early as 1910.

The zipper was invented in the 1800s, but the design we recognize today was not patented until 1914. A competing jeans producer, Lee, seems to have been the first to use them. Starting in 1926, Lee made pants with zippers, while Levi's waited until the '50s to begin consistently using them in their manufacturing process.

However, the familiar nine-ounce denim, just like Jacob Davis used to order from Levi Strauss in the mid 1800s, remained unchanged. In 1915, Levi's changed fabric suppliers from Amoskeag to Cone Denim.

Prewashed jeans made their debut in 1936, but they did not become mainstream until the 1960s. Previously, cowboys would jump into their horses' water troughs with their new jeans on. The pants conformed themselves to the wearer's body when they dried.

Despite the difficult economic conditions that took place during the 1920s and '30s, there were also many advances and new inventions that spurred changes in denim manufacturing.

One of the most innovative companies during the interwar period was the H.D. Lee Mercantile Co. In 1913, Lee released their *Union-All*, which was a combination of pants and jacket that covered the wearer from neck to ankles. It instantly became a hit among laborers such as miners, mechanics, farmers and factory workers. Even chauffeurs used them.

Demand for the overalls was so great that Lee expanded, building factories in Missouri, Kansas, Indiana, New Jersey, Minnesota, and a distribution facility in California.

The name Union-All stems from the fact that Lee's employees belonged to the United Garment Workers of America. In 1916, Lee began using union tickets in all of their clothes, but there are examples of union tickets being used even earlier.

The Los Angeles-based Brownstein, Newmark and Louis placed union tickets in their *Stronghold* pants in 1901. As already described, usage of union labels was a way for companies to appear responsible and politically correct, but the label was additionally used to state the garment's origin.

In 1917, Lee became the first company to market their garments in a major national newspaper advertising campaign. The following year, Levi's launched its counterpart to Lee's Union-All: *Freedom-Alls*, which were a garment for women. It resembled a tunic or robelike outfit that was specifically designed to give women freedom of movement and allow them to avoid contemporary tight, uncomfortable clothes. However, Levi's was still only known on the West Coast at this time and Lee ended up taking a larger market share.

Another of Lee's innovations was the *Buddy Lee doll* released in 1920. It was a ceramic figurine dressed in Lee's clothes that appeared in department store windows everywhere. The various dolls wore different garments, making these dolls new and innovative for the period. Today, Buddy Lee dolls are coveted and treasured collectibles. There are many examples of these dolls being passed down from one generation to the next.

The vast majority of Buddy Lee dolls depicted white characters, but a few black characters, called

Black Magic, were also manufactured. Today, these Black Magic dolls are extremely rare.

In 1925, Lee launched its latest invention: *Jelt Denim*. Twisted wire was incorporated to make the denim fabric lighter and more durable than regular denim. It was even softer and more comfortable to wear. They marketed the fabric in many ways, including a staged steamroller running over a pair of Jelt jeans – a bit of a gimmick perhaps – but the jeans held up.

Jelt was a big trend in the 1920s and '30s.

Yet another variation of denim, named *chambray*, appeared between 1910 and 1920. Like Jelt, chambray was softer to wear than regular denim and thinner, almost like muslin, leading to it being extensively used by many, including marines serving in World War II.

In 1939, H.D. Lee Mercantile Co. celebrated fifty years of business. At the time, they were the world's largest manufacturer of work clothing based in the United States.

Virtually every region of the country boasted its own waist overalls manufacturers. Hamilton Carhartt was active in Detroit from 1884 onwards. The Neustadter Brothers launched their popular brand, *Boss of the Road*, in Northern California just before 1900. *Osh-Kosh B'Gosh* overalls were made in Oshkosh, Wisconsin starting in 1895. Hudson Overall Co., later known as Blue Bell and creator of *Wrangler* jeans, opened up shop in Greensboro, North Carolina, in 1904. Eloesser-Heynemann had factories around San Francisco and Los Angeles, California, and Portland, Oregon. Their flagship was the brand *Can't Bust 'Em*, which was very similar to Levi's early pants. In 1925, Eloesser-Heynemann referred to their waist overalls as *Frisko Jeens* because jeans were what customers called waist overalls. However, it would take three decades before Levi's officially called their denim pants "jeans".

When workwear denim became popular around the years 1905 – 1910, big chains like Montgomery Ward, Roebuck and Co., JC Penney, and Chicago's Sears launched their own brands and started selling them across the nation. These chains chose to subcontract their jeans production, using manufacturers around the country instead of attempting it in-house.

One of the reasons that jeans became so popular was due to strong product marketing. It was no longer just miners who used them but also forest workers, mechanics, and railway workers laying track throughout the country.

As previously stated, to get from east to west across the U.S., one had to travel by ship around South America or go overland through Panama. The only other alternative was to travel on foot or by wagon along the lengthy and dangerous route across the continent. By 1869, the first transcontinental line opened, making it possible to go by railway from New York City all the way to San Francisco.

In the early 1900s, the railway network was built out further, adding four other lines in the United States and one in Canada. This growth provided more routes to the Pacific coast and granted access to all the land in between. Previously isolated areas of the country began to expand and many small towns and cities arose. New farmland also quickly appeared. Likewise, new mineral discoveries were made and markets emerged for goods from the East Coast. Virtually the entire country was now accessible via train, giving rise to a true national economy for the first time ever.

It wasn't only commerce and community building that benefited from the country's newfound rail transit. Tourism soared since it was now possible for people on the East Coast to travel all the way to California and back in a few weeks – something that was unimaginable before.

J.D. Spreckels, one of California's early railway entrepreneurs, may have explained it best: transport determines how people move about; but before you can sell someone on a new place to live, you have to first show them that they can get there quickly, comfortably, and above all, inexpensively.

The railway system would eventually exceed Spreckels' expectations. It was expensive at first, but prices fell drastically as competition increased between private train operators.

Shawnee, Oklahoma, was a significant and well-established rail transport hub in the early 1900s, a place where commerce flourished and many workers were in desperate need of waist overalls. In 1903, the Shawnee Garment Manufacturing Company was founded. It sewed waist overalls for railway workers. Boasting a workforce of more than one hundred employees, they sewed denim overalls for workers on the Choctaw Railroads.

The jeans company later changed its name to the Round House Manufacturing Co., and business was good. In 1910, the company moved to larger premises due to increasing demand. The rail industry was expanding and denim was needed more than ever.

As the railway continued to sprawl across the U.S., the cowboy way of life slowly died out. The emergence of rail and telegraph lines meant there was a decreasing demand for postal delivery by rider or horse-drawn carriage. After the first cowboy feature film debuted in 1914, cowboys, over the next twenty years, were gradually relegated to the realm of fiction. But denim companies couldn't have been happier. For example, Levi's capitalized on this by showcasing cowboys in their advertising, causing millions of moviegoers to observe their favorite western stars dressed in jeans.

And so spread the reputation of jeans.

Few outside of California had seen a pair of denim jeans prior to this time. The attention film gave to denim raised its status with the general public as fans wanted to dress like their favorite movie stars and own a pair of jeans.

But one must not forget that these were still economically stagnant times. A worker during the 1920s and '30s mended his work clothes instead of buying new ones because most had no disposable income. The owner repaired his jeans every time they were damaged. Astonishingly, this could lead to jeans being repaired after each use. It was not uncommon for seams to be reinforced several times. Pocket openings, especially, needed constant attention. Some were resewn so many times that they completely changed in appearance. Old jeans were used to patch up jeans currently in use. Literally anything was used to prolong the life of a worker's denim during this era.

The car's headlights burn holes in the night as they bend with the road. The paved lines on the asphalt flash past at a brisk pace. It's pitch black outside, but the horizon is turning into light, like a halo over the desert landscape.

Las Vegas.

An hour later, the team whizzes past the Vegas suburbs scattered along the highway and enters the city. The contrast of the desert's silence and darkness could not be greater. Here the streetlights, cars, motorcycles, buses, traffic lights and billboards are screaming in neon. There are people everywhere. Many are here on vacation while others are on their way to or from work. Simply put, it's a big city – one that never seems to rest.

Mike drives the car to a hotel parking lot and stops. He turns off the engine and steps out. Walking between the other parked cars, he makes his way to the hotel office.

Inside, there is a man in his fifties watching a little TV that hangs on the wall behind the counter. They are greeted by the man as they enter, but he doesn't divert his gaze from the talk show. He finally turns to the group as they reach the counter, flashes a sleepy smile and asks if they want to check-in.

△ A BOLL WEEVIL attacks a cotton flower. The photo was taken in the 1930s during the Great Depression.

STRONGHOLD 1899–1911

Stronghold pants from Brownstein, Newmark & Louis. The company was – and still is –
a Los Angeles-based company. The jeans are from sometime between 1899 and 1911, the latter
of which was the year P. A. Newmark left the company and sold his interest to his partners.
The company subsequently changed its name to the Brownstein-Louis Company.

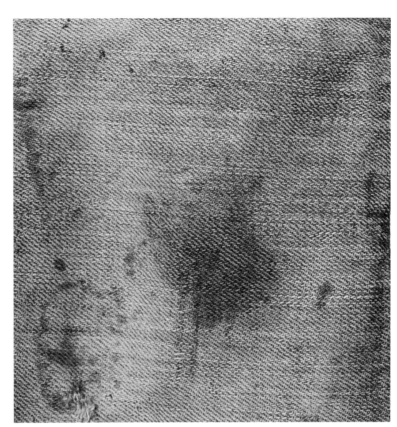

▽ THE MOST COMMON LOCATION of *union tickets* was on the inside of the pockets. Here it is attached inside the back pocket of a pair of jeans.

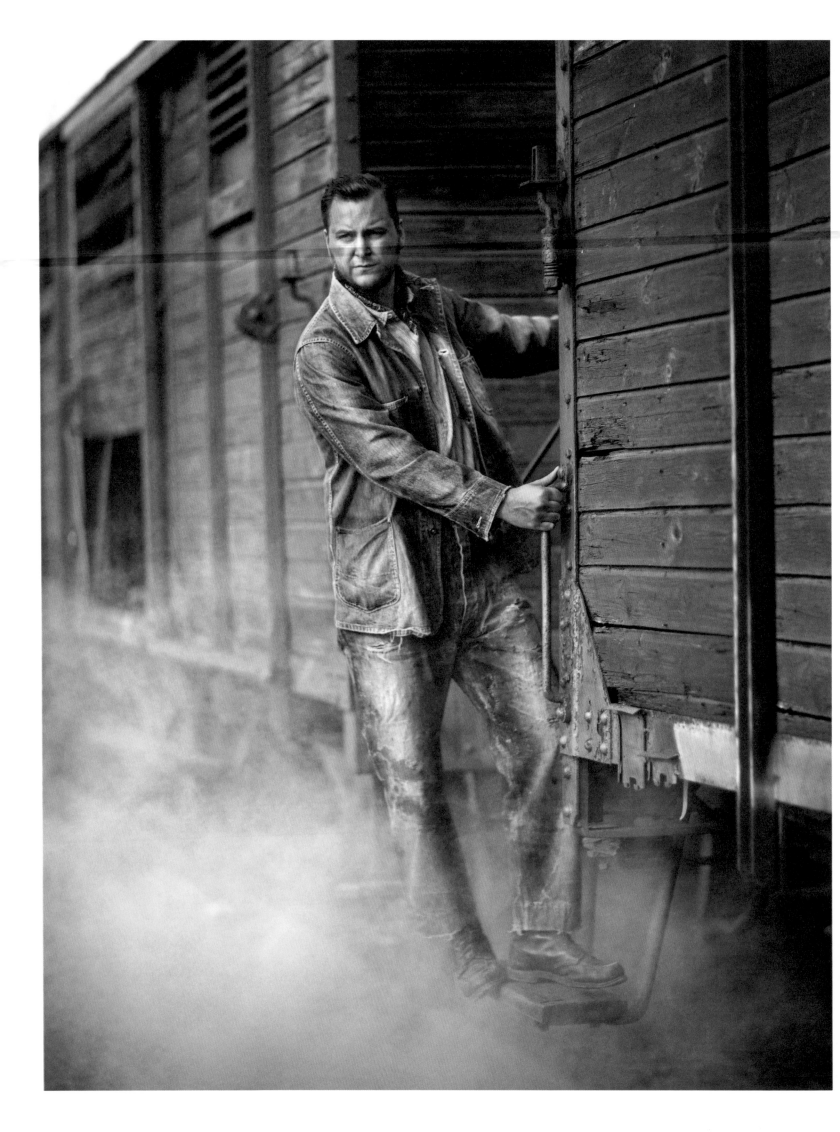

NEUSTADTER BROTHERS
BOSS OF THE ROAD, LOT X 1920

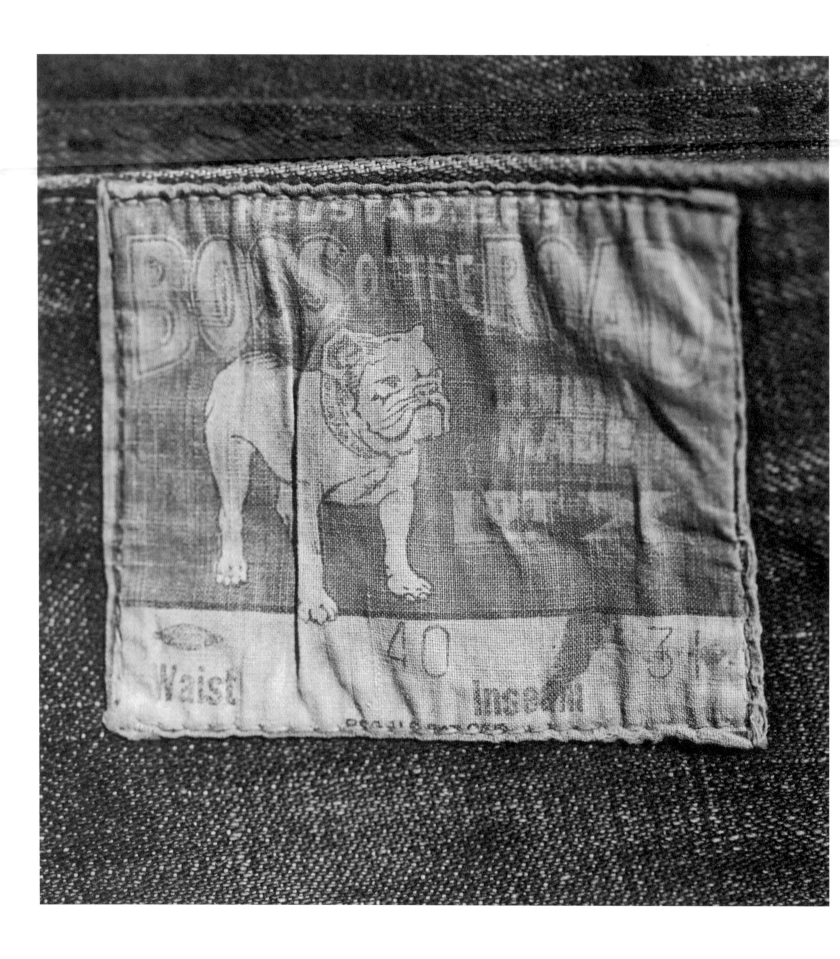

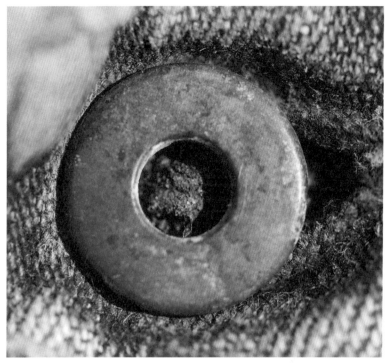

1861/1862-1946
HEYNEMANN & COMPANY
FAMILY TREE

1861 1862
HEYNEMANN & COMPANY
SAN FRANCISCO

Can't bust 'em waist overalls 1879

Patent for reinforcements at the knees 1881

1881
H. HEYNEMANN & CO

1883
HEYNEMANN & COMPANY

Returning to the original name

Eloesser - Heynemann uses Charles A. Jones patent in its Can't bust 'em jeans after 1900

1883
ELOESSER - HEYNEMANN

1932
BUYS OUT NEUSTADTER BROTHERS

Eloesser - Heynemann - owner of the brand Boss Of The Road 1932

1946
ELOESSER - HEYNEMANN BOUGHT BY H.D. LEE CO.

Your Money's Worth — You Know It

Boss of the Road Overalls hand you value that counts — in work-service, in work-comfort, in workmanship.

Loose-cut and full-fashioned so as to meet every strain, twist or pull. Over-sized where the tug hits hardest. That's why they stand the gaff longer—why they give you a new slant on overall value and clothes-economy.

Look for the Bull Dog on the label. It is your protection. Never has this trade mark meant so much to you as it does today.

Buy them from your local dealer

NEUSTADTER BROS.

San Francisco   Portland

Toughest indigo denim—best union workmanship.

Big, swinging pockets—roomy but not baggy

Double-stitched seams; hold-fast, patent buttons

Giant Bar Pocket Stay—prevents pocket ripping

High cut from crotch to waist insures perfect fit.

Wide cut legs—so you can wear 'em comfortably over woolen pants.

H.D. LEE MERCANTILE CO.
CHAMBRAY SHIRT 1930

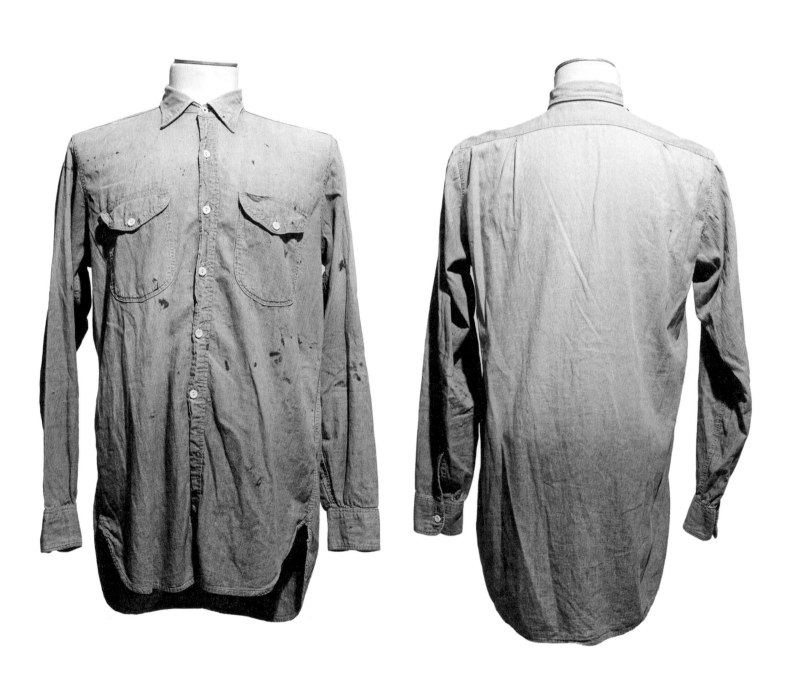

GIBRALTAR TRIPLE STITCH 1910—20

Gibraltar was a trademark owned by the Butler Brothers. The men behind the company were brothers Charles, Edward and George Butler. Together they had started a business that would become one of America's most successful. They came up with the idea to sell bulk goods to retailers using catalogs. Their clients then received the ordered goods through the mail.

In 1877, the brothers opened their first store in Boston. Two years later, they moved to Chicago. In time, they would expand into several major cities around the country.

Gibraltar was a brand of overalls – what they called the *apron overall*, which is the equivalent of dungarees. But the Butler Brothers even made denim shirts like this, with

original wooden buttons. The length of the sleeves, however, is not original – as the former owner has cut them off. The chambray fabric is from Amoskeag. The garment dates to sometime between 1910 and 1920.

In their advertisements, Gibraltar emphasized that they could keep prices low because they had their own jeans manufacturing and therefore were not dependent on middlemen. They also advertised: "When we specify a weight it is exactly as specified." However, Gibraltar's main slogan was probably "triple stitched", which meant that all areas of their clothing where there was the biggest potential for breakage were reinforced with triple stitching.

H.D. LEE CO. HICKORYSTRIPE CAP 1960

It says "Reading Lines" on the cap. It's the logo for the Reading Company, RDG, a major railway company in Pennsylvania. Reading Co. was one of America's most successful companies and made large profits from transporting coal, or *anthracite*, from the coal region of northeastern Pennsylvania to other states. But things would soon take a turn for the worse. After World War II began, the coal began to run out. During the 1970s, bankruptcy became inevitable and in 1976 the company was purchased by Conrail.

Train service between Philadelphia and Reading has a rich history. In fact, it is one of America's oldest train lines. Opening back in 1842, it was also the first line in the country to have double tracks. The railway company employees and the countless workers who built the tracks all wore denim clothing on the job. Obviously, Lee got that contract. The small patch just above the screen reveals that the cap is made of sanforized denim and was, like everything else made by Lee since the 20th century, union made. The cap dates from the early 60's.

JC PENNEY PAY DAY 1930

It was common during the Great Depression of the 1930s to mend and patch one's garments. These jeans belonged to a corn farmer from Missouri who had a wife and children. They are a pair of Pay Day jeans, one of JC Penney's brands. The garment is made of sanforized denim and is *union made*. Pay Day's slogan was "The Best Known Name In The Overall World".

If you take a look at the garment seams you can see that the corn farmer's wife has reinforced most of them – not just once, but several times. In addition, she's sewn around all the pocket openings. She's reinforced some so many times that they have even changed shape.

On the back, she's mended his pants around the corners on both sides, and used right and left backsides from other discarded jeans.

It is interesting that she's adapted the pants to her husband's work as a farmer. Obviously, her husband didn't need a tool pocket, so she closed it – probably after tiring of hearing him complain about dirt and debris that gathered there. She even removed the hammer holder – most likely because it got caught on everything.

Since the corn farmer did not need to store anything at thigh-height on the pants, one can clearly see that he used the breast pocket instead, wearing it out substantially in the process.

Another detail is that visible traces of the orange selvedge can be seen in the seam on the sides of the jeans.

His wife describes how she used to patch up the waist overalls: "In the beginning, I fixed them every time they broke. And at the end, every time they were used."

H.D. LEE MERCANTILE CO. TIN CANS

Many may not know that Lee began his career by selling "dry goods" and food in tin cans. But with the Second World War, the company moved more and more towards garment manufacturing exclusively. To emphasize its new, slimmed-down direction, the company decided in 1943 to shorten its name. "Mercantile" had run its course and the company became known by the name it is called today: H.D. Lee Company.

BUDDY LEE BLACK MAGIC

Black Magic is the name of the black version of the doll advertising Buddy Lee jeans, one of the brands manufactured by the H.D. Lee Company. Black Magic's history and purpose are shrouded in mystery, but like its paler-skinned Buddy Lee Doll predecessors, Black Magic was probably made back in the 1920s. However, there are some people that date the doll to the 40's.

Buddy Lee dolls appeared in advertisements and in store windows across America and garnered immediate success. Sometimes the dolls were sold or given away as gifts during special business promotions. The dolls' main purpose was nonetheless to introduce Lee's new products.

At first, the Buddy Lee doll was dressed only in overalls, but soon it started to be fitted with shirts and caps. All in all, the Buddy Lee doll had seventeen different outfits, but the Black Magic doll seems to have had only a single outfit consisting of mechanic's overalls and cap that had Black Magic's name on it.

The dolls, regardless of color, were made from a composite of sawdust, wood flour, corn flour, glue and resin, starting from its debut in 1921 all the way to 1948. The dolls were twelve and a half inches high. In 1949, the dolls started to be made out of plastic instead, and grew to thirteen inches high. Gem Toy Company was the company behind the dolls.

In 1962 or 1963, the Buddy Lee dolls' time was over and production was shut down. After years of recognition, Buddy exited his run as a highly regarded cult figure.

As for Black Magic's reputation, it remains unclear.

Debbie Behan Garrett, author of many books including 2003's *The Definitive Guide to Collecting Black Dolls*, says that it is uncertain whether Black Magic was manufactured after 1948. An expert in black dolls and also an avid blogger on the subject, Behan Garrett says that, historically, black dolls were meant to be demeaning, and mocked colored people. The dolls were disproportional and had extreme, impersonal traits. But later, black dolls would increasingly begin to emulate the people they portrayed.

In fact, this was very much the case even with white dolls. They evolved from simple, rustic dolls to ones with more and more chiseled and detailed facial features. In large part, it was due to the fact that the technology behind the production got better and better.

But when it comes to Black Magic, there are still reasons to question some.

Debbie Behan Garrett says that even though the name of Black Magic was a way for the company to distinguish the black dolls from the white Buddy Lee dolls, the name is still something of a mystery. It is not just stereotypical, but also alludes to *black magic*, which, according to The Oxford Dictionary, means "invoking evil spirits for evil purposes". Behan Garrett reasons, "It certainly should not be associated with a doll of any color, especially one used for advertising purposes."

So why did Lee chose to manufacture Black Magic? If it is as Debbie Behan Garrett argues – that companies claim that black dolls do not sell – then whatever reason lies behind it is even more remarkable. Unfortunately there is no information out there regarding Black Magic. Perhaps the black Lee doll's story is lost forever?

But what can't be denied is that the doll really was manufactured at one point in time. You can see it here.

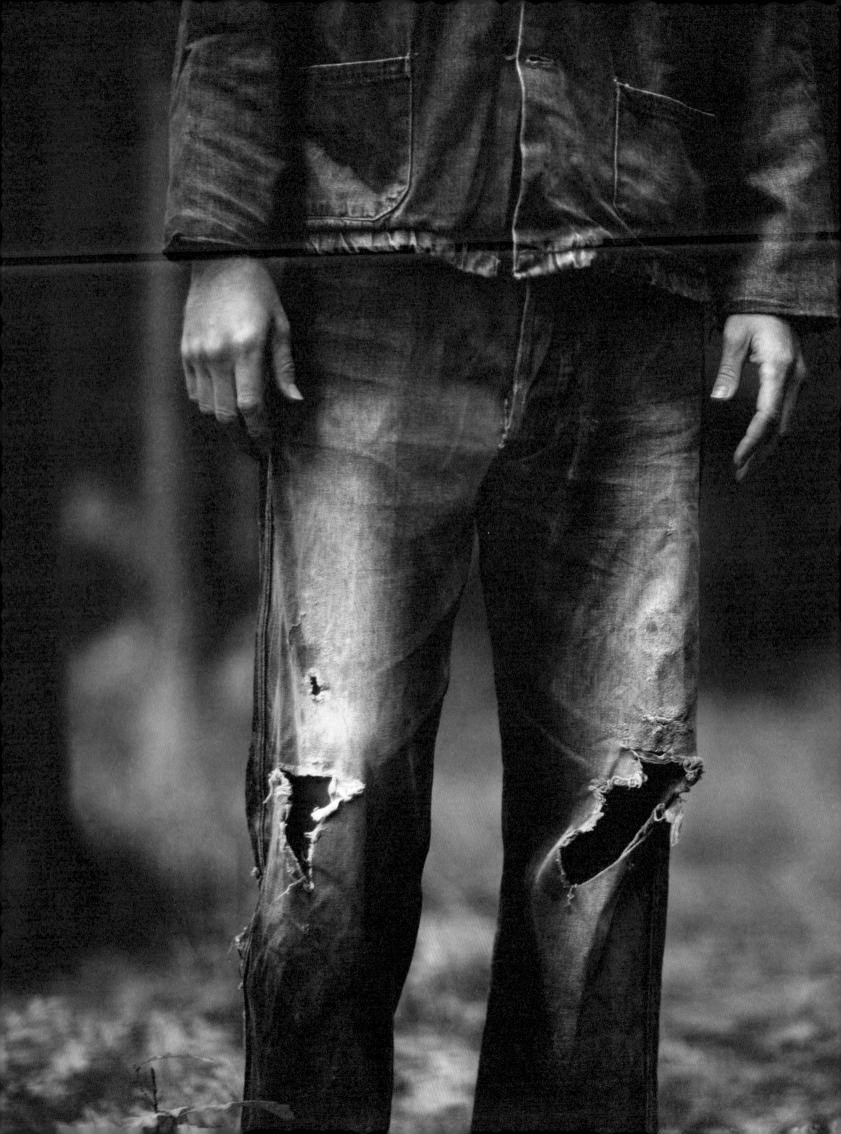

LUMBERJACK

"Lumberjack" is the old term for a woodsman. The term refers to a bygone time when all work in the forest was done by hand with axes and large handsaws.

The job itself was difficult and very dangerous. Actually, it is by far the most dangerous industry today. In 2008, the forestry industry in the United States had an unimaginable thirty percent more fatalities than any other industry.

The stories and myths of lumberjacks are many. Quite a few are certainly exaggerated, but one thing is for sure: it was a life that demanded men to have the right stuff. Lumberjacks had a reputation for being hard working and hard drinking. In the small camps that arose in the middle of the woods grew a special, manly culture. It was a nomadic life, so woodcutters followed work wherever it led.

In 1906, logging reached its apex. At that time there were about five hundred thousand lumberjacks. Many of these were immigrants, mostly from the Scandinavian countries.

Jeans were a necessary garment for lumberjacks when working in the forests. The brand of jeans was not considered important in the early 1900s. At that time, it was still the weight of the denim and the quality that was most important factor. Most jean companies had patches with illustrations. Animals were a common motif.

But why did they use illustrations instead of words on their patches?

Now, over a hundred years later, it is perhaps tempting to look back on this time and assume that the people were illiterate, and that was the reason why denim companies used images in their marketing. But actually, the literacy rate of the time was very high – especially among the Scandinavians, who were schooled Bible reading.

The jeans in the pictures are from approximately 1900 to 1910 – when the forest industry was at its peak in the United States. The names of the brands were sometimes very similar: Boss Overall, Boss of the Road, The Boss, Big Boss, and others.

If one is allowed to speculate, jeans brand names seemingly wanted to symbolize strength, power and masculinity.

During the era, lumberjacks were epitomes of all of those qualities – they were the tough men of the time.

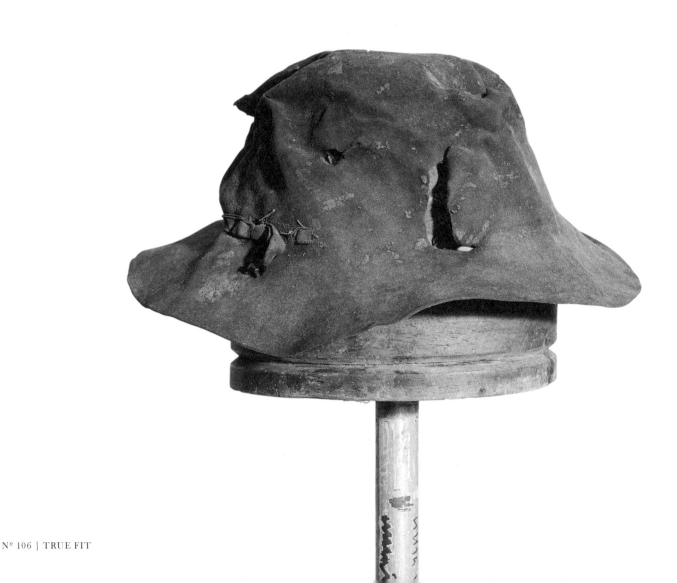

M.E.S. & CO. IDEAL
BOSS-OVERALL NUMBER ONE 1910

LEVI'S 501 1937—41

The first Levi's with the red tab were introduced in 1936. Earlier surface rivets were
now hidden under a layer of denim and became furniture friendly "hidden rivets".

IN TIMES OF WAR

"Viktor? Viktor?"
An outside voice penetrates straight into his dream as a hand
falls on his shoulder. Viktor abruptly wakes up. Mike looms over Viktor
in the hotel room and intently shakes him. There's urgency in his eyes.
"Time to go", he says.

It's still dark outside as Mike turns around and starts packing their bags. Viktor, startled and angry, tells him to relax. Mike is persistent, "No, we gotta go. Leave the hotel. Now!"

Viktor stretches out his hand to check the time on his cell phone, but Mike beats him to it and announces it's half past two in the morning. Viktor has only slept an hour. He sighs and throws the sheets off the bed as he sits up. Fatigue plagues his every muscle and joint after so much time in the mines.

"Do you realize how comfortable this bed is?" Viktor says, rubbing his face.

Mike asks Viktor to come into the bathroom so he can witness what's happened there.

Viktor reluctantly obeys and surveys what's occurred.

"Okay, this is a problem."

The entire bathroom floor is flooded with dirty, rusty-red water.

When someone in the group finds a pair of jeans, they almost look like roots – twisted, wrinkled, and very brown. It's only after they've been washed that the native blue color comes to life.

Mike explains that he was so excited that he couldn't wait until he got home to wash his newfound jeans. He usually performs this ritual with his wife Charla at home, but this time he decided to do it himself – in the hotel room. Unfortunately, the drain clogged up while rinsing off the jeans. Now there is water flowing out of the bathroom.

Fifteen minutes later, they've checked out of the hotel and are driving away in Mike's car. They look at each other and burst out laughing. Mike is laughing so hard that he must wipe the tears from his eyes to see where he's driving.

In a cloud of dust, they leave the warzone behind.

After the Great Depression of the 1930s, the world was thrown into an even darker period: World War II. It was only a matter of time before the U.S. would be drawn into the war and it became inevitable after the attack on Pearl Harbor in December 1941. The U.S. government immediately mobilized the country's resources and realized that there was a great need for clothing for the soldiers.

The U.S. government probably ordered the larger jean companies to start producing garments for the military. Due to the overwhelming sense of solidarity during wartime in America, no company refused. Most important of all were those companies which had the opportunity and the capacity to mass-produce garments. Small businesses also ostensibly tried to pitch in where they could, but sometimes their small size prohibited them. Apparently, the major brands dominated the wartime effort. Lee was one of the companies that participated. It's unknown whether Levi's also participated; however, it is very likely due to their status as one of the biggest brands.

Women took over work in the factories because of the shortage of men during the war. It was women, working overtime, who kept jeans production going throughout these years. Special working uniforms were manufactured for woman.

In addition to traditional "civilian" jeans, manufacturing companies made, as already mentioned, uniforms for the U.S. Army, Navy, and Air Force. There were five different styles of garments manufactured for soldiers. Among them was a complete overall in the style of Lee's Union-Alls. This particular denim garment was used by flight mechanics and many others.

These companies were not allowed to label the military clothing they produced with their own brands, but those who were particularly in the know could identify the different brands based on the seams sewn into the garment and other characteristics.

The same ban applied to buttons. Previously, every company had its own branded buttons. But the war brought many restrictions. All jeans manufacturers used the same type of button: the *leaf logo button*.

These buttons were made of different materials. The U.S. Army had buttons made of zinc on their garments while the Navy used bakelite buttons. Bakelite was the first type of hard plastic to be manufactured. Leaf logo buttons were not new to World War II soldiers. They were already used on jeans during the 1920s. Most likely, the leaf logo was a standard button that was widely available. It was potentially used by smaller denim brands that could not afford to produce their own branded buttons.

As previously mentioned, the country made great efforts to cut costs during the war, resulting in a general shortage of consumer goods. Likewise, the manufacture and availability of fabric was not as extensive as in normal times. This resulted in a clear deterioration of denim garment quality compared to what was available before and after the war. It was not only seen in American soldiers' clothing, but was consistent with overall denim production.

Chambray denim was partly used in Navy uniforms during the war, probably because it was more comfortable to wear than regular denim. But chambray is also thinner and lighter, which likely meant there was a cost savings compared to using regular denim. Chambray is also less durable, but the wartime effort dictated that quality was sacrificed for low cost.

Cost cutting measures were even prevalent in the civilian world. For instance, overall buttons were no longer placed on pants regardless of the brand – and they would never return.

The cinch strap on the back of the jeans was abandoned too – and never came back.

The number of buttons used on the fly was not exempt from cost-cutting either. Levi's used one less button on their fly, creating a larger gap between those that remained.

All brands also removed the rivets in the small coin pocket. The remaining rivets were no longer made of copper, but lead-coated with copper paint.

Everything that was non-functional was removed during the war years, whether it was fabric, buttons, rivets, or wire. Any modification or elimination that could save money was put in place. Decorative elements, such as Levi's arcuate stitch on the back pockets, are another example of something that was removed. However, this arcuate stitch was an established identity mark for Levi's and the company opted to paint it on their jeans instead.

Lee, which had a patent for the inner lining of their pockets, retained their back pocket seam. The reason was that this seam was the only way to fasten together the extra layers of fabric. The pockets would not work without it. But all the other denim brands that did not have this feature had to remove the stitching on their back pockets.

There seems to have been no strictly defined jeans design during the war years. Variations were many, and departures from past patterns and practices were commonplace. One theory is that the jeans manufacturers simply used what they had in stock until supplies ran out. After that, they used anything that was available to them. Clearly rationing was in full swing.

In these difficult times, competition became even more cutthroat between jean manufacturers.

Levi's sued several brands for plagiarism during the war years. Other brands such as Lee and Blue Bell (Wrangler) applied an arcuate stitch on their back pockets, infuriating Levi's. Why were the other brands so interested in imitating Levi's? Perhaps Levi's design was so appealing that they couldn't resist.

A more likely explanation is that, in these financially strained times, competitors tried to steal some of Levi's market share.

Viktor hugs Mike, then Cory and Russ. The mood is upbeat and goodbyes are not needed. They all know they will see each other again when Viktor returns.

Viktor shows his boarding pass at the airport checkpoint and gets in line to go through security. When it's his turn, he puts his bag, jacket, and shoes on the belt and steps through the metal detector.

The airport security agent rewinds the conveyor belt and x-rays Viktor's hand luggage again. She decides to do a more thorough check.

The security agent opens Viktor's bag and leans over it. The bag is filled with old relics from the desert and various markets. Viktor worries the security agent is about to poke around and damage the items without regard to the condition and value of the fragile relics. He can't help but imagine thousands of dollars going up in smoke right before his eyes.

To his relief, and without touching a thing, the security agent simply raises her eyebrows and lets him go.

Viktor takes a deep breath while walking to his gate – that was a close call.

A little while later, he sits looking out the small window at America slowly sweeping by underneath him. The plane rises toward its cruising altitude, but he can still make out the flow of cars along the road below. They are like little oxygen atoms in a nationwide network of veins and arteries.

He is on his way home again – a long flight to Stockholm. He is tired, but happy.

As soon as the plane reaches cruising altitude and the "fasten seat belt" sign turns off, the staff starts to serve dinner. They repeat the same empty words and phrases as they work through the aisles of passengers.

Through his small window, Viktor catches small glimpses of America between the clouds outside. He begins to ponder.

World War II changed jeans forever. It's a fact. Many of the changes that were made during the war years would continue on afterwards, but not all. Some may question why the quality used in denim before the war did not return afterwards, especially when the economy eventually recovered.

One possible answer is that, thanks to the American soldiers' abundant use of jeans, the relatively new garment spread throughout the world. People from other countries became interested in denim, which in turn increased demand for jeans starting at the end of the 1940s and into the 1950s.

But the most likely answer Viktor has to this question is that jeans companies, despite various cost-cutting measures and downgrades, noticed their jeans actually sold just as well as before – and maybe even better.

U.S. NAVY DECK JACKET 1940

The pictures show a jacket that was used by the U.S. Navy during World War II. The insignia confirms that the original owner was a "Corpsman 3rd Class".

The red cross shows that the soldier belonged to the "Hospital Corps" as a medic. The red, V-shaped ribbon stands for 3-8 years, and refers to the number of years the soldier has been in the service. Had he served more than 8 years, he would have two red ribbons. The band or bands are also the basis for the Navy's structured pay system, which was based on the rank the soldier had. The higher the rank, the higher the salary. A soldier could also receive a pay raise within his own rank by being awarded medals. Each medal earned increased the soldier's wage by a couple dollars per month.

The word "Doc" on the front appears bleached out and was a common nickname for medics during the war. Medics had such an important and supportive role in warfare that defacements of the uniform like this were generally overlooked by superiors. Soldiers were dependent on medics and Hospital Corpsmen to save their lives if they were injured in the field, so the presence of *Doc* was good for the men's morale.

U.S. NAVY DUNGAREE PANTS 1940

ARCUATE STITCHES

▽ BOSS-OVERALL NUMBER ONE

▽ H.D. LEE COMPANY

"Rely on Reliance"

We'll *always* celebrate
THE FOURTH!

One hundred thirty million free American men and women will see to that! Ten thousand men and women workers in 19 Reliance plants are supplying parachutes for men and matériel, garments for the Army and Navy, and essential apparel for men and women workers at home. Reliance can be relied upon to produce for war, as well as for peace!

Illustrated: Big Yank Work Shirt,' Happy Home Frock and Ensenada Shirt and Slacks

Reliance
BIG YANK

RELIANCE MANUFACTURING COMPANY
212 W. Monroe St., Chicago, Ill. • New York Offices: 200 Fifth Ave., 1350 Broadway

MAKERS OF *Big Yank Work Clothing* • *Aywon Shirts* • *Ensenada Shirts and Slacks* • *Universal Pajamas*
Happy Home and Kay Whitney Frocks • *No-Tare Shorts* • *Parachutes for Men and Matériel*

Beacon Plant

when that
Great Day
comes!

You'll wake up some morning with the last belligerent Jap gone the way of his ignoble ancestors. The shout of "Heil Hitler" will no longer threaten slavery and death for free people.

To hasten that day you accepted rationing of the miles you drive, the very food on your table, the fuel to heat your home in winter. *This, is America at war!*

From time to time, you may have found your Lee Dealer temporarily short of your favorite Lee Work Clothes. But you have been patient because you knew that somehow, the materials for the particular Lee you wanted at the moment had gone to clothe a soldier.

Until "The Great Day" comes, Lee Work Clothes will continue to fight on many fronts. In the meantime your Lee Dealer is receiving new shipments of Lee Work Clothes as often and in whatever quantities available after military needs have been met.

Now, as always, you'll find LEE is your best buy in work clothes. If your Lee Dealer doesn't have exactly the garment you want, he may have a different one suitable for your purpose. If you should happen to hit one of those rare times when he can't supply you at all, you'll be glad you waited a few days for the garment with this unconditional guarantee, "Your Lee garment must *look better, fit better, wear longer* than any garment you've ever worn . . . or you get a new one free or your money back."

Highest Quality
UNION MADE
Lee
Work Clothes and
Industrial Uniforms

**JELT DENIM OVERALLS • UNION-ALLS • MATCHED
SHIRTS AND PANTS • WHIPCORDS • DUNGAREES
COWBOY PANTS • INDUSTRIAL UNIFORMS**
Copr. 1943, The H. D. Lee Company, Inc., Kansas City, Mo. • Trenton N. J.
South Bend, Ind. • Minneapolis, Minn. • San Francisco, Calif. • Salina, Kans.

IN PEACE OR WAR — THE LARGEST SELLING LINE OF ITS KIND IN AMERICA

LEVI'S S501XX 1944—46

During World War II, Levi's painted their *arcuate stitch* on their trouser pockets because of rationing. The arcuate stitch would fade away after only few washes, but it was important that it was in place when the new Levi's jeans were bought because it was strongly associated with their brand.

Another interesting detail is that the pockets were made from different materials during the war. The general lack of materials meant that what was available was put to use – so sometimes the cloth used to form the inside of the pocket was green, and sometimes it was striped. They could look very different and all industry standards were abandoned during this period.

Jeans firms were forced to make more compromises during the war years. Since they could not use their own buttons on their own brands, a default button was used instead: the *leaf logo button*, also called the *laurel leaf button*.

The laurel wreath's design can be traced back to 776 BC, when the winners of the ancient Olympic Games in contemporary Greece were adorned with a crown made of laurel leaves. Ever since then, the laurel wreath has been a powerful symbol of strength, victory and glory, in both sports and academic studies. Some claim that the laurel wreath was the precursor to the royal crowns.

Indeed, one can trace the laurel wreath further back than that. In Greek mythology, Apollo, son of Zeus, is often depicted with a laurel wreath around his head. The myth tells us that Apollo was in love with a nymph, Daphne, who transformed herself into a laurel tree to escape his persistent courtship. He broke a twig of the tree, wrapped it around his head and declared the tree sacred. To wear a laurel wreath is therefore tantamount to honoring the god Apollo.

It is unclear why they chose laurel leaf buttons for soldiers' garments during World War II and not smooth, neutral buttons. But given the laurel wreath symbolism – and the fact that American soldiers were on their way to Europe to fight against the Third Reich – perhaps it was an attractive and much needed symbol. Or maybe the laurel leaf button was used as a lucky charm.

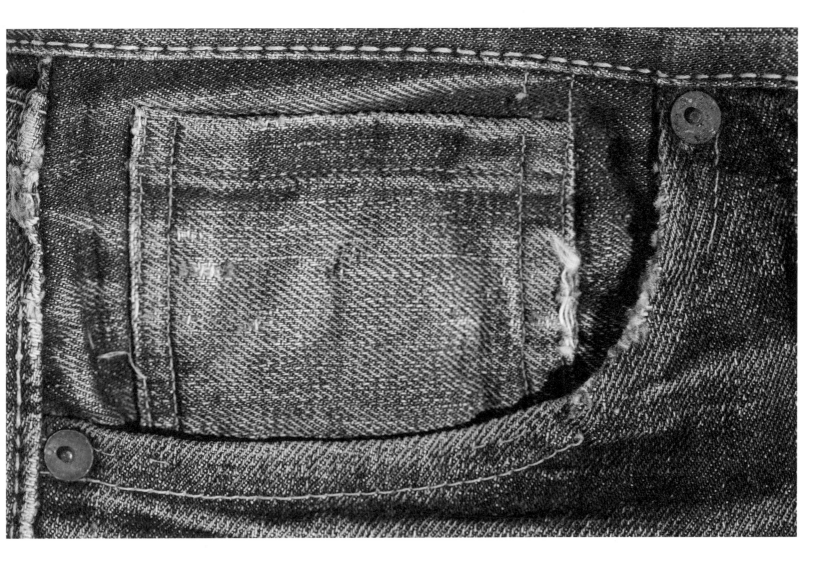

U.S. ARMY PULLOVER 1930

Denim produced for the war industry was highly regulated. On each label in each garment the following had to be specified: the garment's weight in "yards per pound" or, alternatively, in "ounces per square yard". The fabric width was to be between twenty-eight to twenty-nine inches. In addition, it was to indicate whether the garment was "preshrunk" or not. Random quality control was performed on "preshrunk" clothes, and if they shrank more than two per cent they were considered to be "unshrunk".

War models were either "first quality" or "second quality", which was also called "seconds". The first quality category was for garments that met all of the criteria that the Armed Forces required – and the list of details was long. Seconds were garments that did not meet the quality standards, and therefore were considered to be of substandard quality.

The picture shows an Army jacket from sometime between 1930 and 1940. If it is of first quality or is a "second" is unclear.

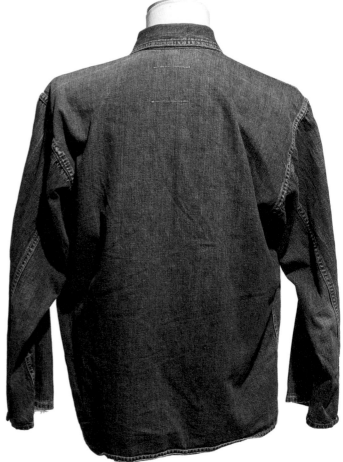

U.S. ARMY COVERALL JACKET 1940

U.S. NAVY LAUNDRY BAG 1940

△ AMERICAN ARMY SOLDIERS at the beginning of World War II received bags made of denim that were used to carry laundry and other personal belongings. Unfortunately, denim laundry bags became too expensive to produce and were quickly taken out of production. This army bag from World War II is in poor condition. There are tears, pinholes and bleached marks. Valiant attempts to mend the garment can be seen throughout. But in general, the denim is not particularly damaged and has retained most of its indigo color. The bag also has intact gromets on each side of the opening, and the white cotton cords used to close it are fully usable. Inside is a pale, almost illegible army label. It is a *U.S. Army WW2 GI Denim Laundry Barracks Bag*, worn out by all it's been through.

△ U.S. MARINE CORP BOOTS from World War II.

△ FRANK CURRY a.k.a "The Manhattan Matador".

GRAB THE BULL BY THE HORNS

Rodeo Clown Frank Curry had just finished his show.
He bowed to the laughing audience and thanked them for the applause.
He was the Manhattan Matador,
one of the world's most well-known rodeo clowns.

Frank was standing outside the arena, ready and waiting to step in if something were to happen to the next rider. Truth be told, there was rarely a quiet moment in the sport of rodeo. And this suited Frank perfectly.

Inside the fence, the next rider positioned himself on the bull's back with his hand pressed underneath a rope that was tied around the bull's chest. The rider clenched his hand firmly around the rope and held up his other hand. He signaled he was ready.

The rules of rodeo were clear. The contestants would try to remain on the bull's back for eight seconds while holding on with only one hand. If the rider's free hand so much as touched the bull, he was disqualified. The score was calculated based on the rider's skill combined with the number of seconds he managed to stay on the bull's back.

Suddenly, the chute gate opened and the bull jumped out – bucking, butting, and spinning at a furious pace.

Eight seconds is an eternity when riding a bull.

Yet, everything happens in a fraction of a second.

The rider was thrown off in a little more than five seconds. He got slammed down on his back, gets one thigh trampled on, and had the wind knocked out of him. The bull immediately seized the opportunity to inflict more damage. It spun around and butted him right in the chest, pushing him hard against the ground with his horns and his one thousand five hundred pounds of body weight. The bull then lifted the rider up with his horns and threw him as if he were a small toy.

It all happened so fast.

Frank arrived just a few moments later and managed to distract the bull so that it attacked him instead of the helpless rider. Frank's associates were also quick to the scene and soon the bull had focused all its anger on the clowns. The most important task of a rodeo clown is to protect the riders, but the job description also requires them to be funny.

Frank managed to evade the bull as it turned and

attempted to gore him. The audience then laughed at Frank's comical escape as he waved his arms excessively and threw his hat over his shoulder, leading the bull on a wild chase as he ran away.

The bull slowed and refocused to attack the hat. Then it paused and stared as Frank stopped a short distance away. Two other rodeo clowns surrounded the angry bull, but it honed in on Frank. He was the most interesting. Meanwhile, the commentators' voices squawked through the speakers as they announced the rider's total points and current standing in the competition.

Frank waved to the crowd as they screamed and applauded.

Born in New York in 1940, Frank Curry became fascinated at an early age by Manolete, a Mexican bullfighter who was regarded as the world's greatest. As a child, Frank would watch television – a new invention at the time. He was especially drawn to Westerns with Dave Evans, Gene Autry, Roy Rogers and others. He saw rodeo clowns performing in various shows on TV.

In his teens, Frank would go see the rodeo live at Madison Square Garden. There he met rodeo clown idols like The Cajun Kid, Buck LeGrand, and elephant trainer Hugo Schmidt. He knew he had found his calling.

Frank began as a rodeo clown when he was fifteen under the name the Manhattan Matador. He continued as a rodeo clown for eleven years and was the promoter for every rodeo in which he appeared.

Frank later worked as a marketing executive for Ringling Brothers, the well-known American circus company. Additionally, he created and produced the Ronald McDonald Circus. His goal had been to entertain families at an affordable price while providing the best quality and variety possible. It took little time for Frank's dreams to become reality and he ended up producing the Ronald McDonald Circus for over twenty years.

The bull sped towards Frank Curry and lowered its horns into stabbing position. Frank met the bull with the same momentum. He would try performing one of his deadly tricks: jumping over the bull.

He had successfully done it a few times previously – and he would continue to perform the trick throughout his rodeo clown career. However, he was painfully aware each time of the risks involved. Sometimes, Frank didn't get enough lift, poorly judged the physical logistics of the trick, or miscalculated his timing. When this happened, the bull would usually have its way with him, and he ended up butted and gored.

One thing was certain: Frank put his life on the line every time he stepped into a rodeo ring.

He had been hospitalized five times in five different cities, but it was more dangerous when he was young and inexperienced. Later in his career, he would mostly scrape by with nothing but bruising.

Suddenly, the noise of the crowd was gone. Frank heard nothing but the blood in his ears and hooves drumming against the ground. Like a gunshot, the bull charged at him with lowered horns.

Frank mustered up all the power he had and jumped.

"I'm outside", she said into the phone. "Where are you?"

Viktor sat in the airplane on the way to Sweden and thought of his mistake. He felt guilty and somewhat remorseful.

He had been standing outside the gate at Los Angeles International Airport and was just about to board the plane when she had called. It was the museum curator from the Rotterdam Museum in Holland. They had e-mail contact before and she had asked Viktor if she could borrow some vintage jeans from Mike for an exhibition. Since Mike did not want to mail the jeans, he sent Viktor off with several pairs in his luggage. But Viktor had forgotten to take into account the time zone difference. And now the woman from Holland was outside his door – in Stockholm.

Viktor finally caught up with the museum curator when he arrived home the next day. She was a quiet, professional woman in her forties with brown, medium-length hair. She was average height, well dressed, and had nice shoes. She was a stark contrast to Viktor, who had just been camping out in the Nevada desert and had dirt and sand in every crevice. His clothes and belongings were testament to the struggle.

They shook hands and Viktor apologized again for his delay. The curator asked Viktor about his recent expedition as they entered the house. Her heels echoed throughout the staircase going up to Viktor's apartment.

The bull came toward Frank like a runaway freight train. He jumped, saw the horns pass right under his feet, and landed safely on the other side. The bull rushed round to face him, but all that could be heard was the crowd's wild applause and jubilation.

He had done it. Again.

Frank continued to outmaneuver the bull to the crowd's delight and glee. Many of them hardly dared to look – afraid the bull would nevertheless maul Frank. But Frank was talented. He was one of the best rodeo clowns around.

Rodeo life in the 1950s was the only surviving relic

of the old cowboy lifestyle. Cowboys had been relegated to a corner of entertainment and nostalgia. But that didn't mean there wasn't plenty of excitement.

It doesn't get much tougher than rodeo.

There was another aspect to Frank Curry's rodeo clown persona that was interesting.

His clothes.

Rodeo clowns like Frank were among the first to market jeans. His wide pants were actually a pair of *Wrangler Blue Bells*. He wore them with a red scarf around his neck and a striped shirt. His face was painted like a clown, as one would expect.

The Blue Bell Company, which was started by C.C. Hudson, originally made Wrangler. In 1897, when Hudson was only twenty years old, he moved to North Carolina to begin work in the textile industry. He earned twenty-five cents per day sewing on buttons. In 1904, production was down. Hudson and a few colleagues bought some sewing machines, rented a room, and started the Hudson Overall Company.

In 1919, the company changed its name to the Blue Bell Overall Company and opened their first factory that same year.

In 1936, they began selling *Super Big Ben Overalls*. These pants were made with sanforized denim, which is a pre-shrunk denim that shrinks less than one percent after washing. Before this, unsanforized denim was used, which is a type of denim that leads to garment shrinkage of about ten percent. Customers of the day always had to buy their jeans two or three sizes too big in order to make sure they fit after washing. Many customers underestimated shrinkage and quickly lost the fit of their pants. All things considered, sanforized fabric was a godsend for the textile industry and soon became the industry standard.

In 1943, Blue Bell bought Casey Jones Work-Clothes Company and obtained the rights to a little-used known: Wrangler.

Under the new ownership, the Wrangler brand was first named Wrangler Blue Bell. It wasn't until the 1970s that it became the iconic Wrangler.

The word *wrangler* is synonymous with a working cowboy, which was probably a contributing factor in Blue Bell's decision to launch a new jean for cowboys in 1947. The pants went by the name *Wrangler 11MW*. This acronym stood for Men's Western and the jeans were specially designed for cowboys who spent a lot of time in the saddle. The rear pockets were positioned so they would not rub the rider, and the seams were constructed so that they minimized discomfort. The 11MWs even had a button-fly.

Wrangler was the first company to market their jeans using rodeo clowns in the late 1950s. It was innovative advertising for the time.

Another innovation of the era was embroidery on denim jackets and shirts. It became very popular during the late 1950s, and especially in the 1960s. Embroidery was a way for a garment wearer to show others that they belonged to a certain group, such as a particular ranch, or that they attended a specific school.

In all probability, biker gangs borrowed the inspiration for their self-identifying vests from denim embroidery, but they used sewn-on designs instead. It was also popular to just paint the club emblem directly on jackets and vests.

Either way, people started to experiment with clothing at this time and a denim jacket became something more than just a denim jacket.

It was a statement of who you were and where you belonged.

The museum curator leaned over Viktor's old Levi's N° 2's from 1888-89 with an excited expression. It was clear that she had never seen anything like them. She examined them in detail and asked many questions, which Viktor gladly answered.

"May I take a few pictures of them to send to my boss?" she asked with her cell phone ready in one hand. Viktor nodded. She snapped away and sent the pictures to her boss with captions describing the world's oldest pair of N° 2's.

But when she asked if she could borrow the jeans for the exhibition, Viktor said no. He said he had just bought them and was unwilling to part with them so soon.

But this was not the whole truth.

The jeans had cost him dearly – and not just in money. To afford this prized possession, Viktor sold his entire wardrobe and his dining room table, which meant that he and his girlfriend at the time had to eat dinner on the floor. What's more, Viktor worked seven days a week for several months to save up enough money to buy the jeans. By that time, his girlfriend had decided to leave.

Viktor felt that he could not have prioritized anything differently, however. The old N° 2's were an important part of his big puzzle.

WRANGLER BLUE BELL
RODEO CLOWN JEANS 1950

Frank Curry, billed as The Manhattan Matador, was one of the world's top rodeo clowns. He was the owner of these Wrangler jeans at one point in time. Later in his life, he would become the creator and producer of the Ronald McDonald Circus. The two main bandanas on the back were put there by Frank himself, so they are not original. The pants are from the 1950s, and are just one pair of many produced for marketing purposes during that time. Rodeo Clowns were Wranglers "living billboards".

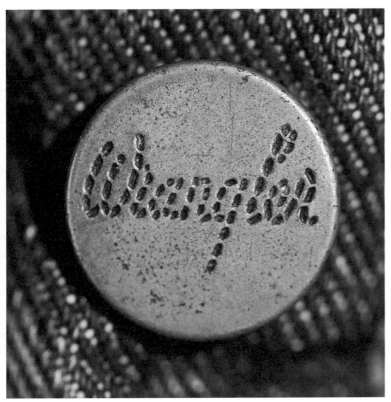

◁ THE PANTS SHE IS WEARING is a pair of Wrangler
Blue Bell 11MW from 1947. The shirt, model 27 MW,
is from the same company and was made in 1952.

RIDE 'EM WRANGLER!

Four out of the last five World Champion rodeo cowboys wear Wrangler jeans, jackets, shirts. They're built for the toughest rodeo, or any kind of everyday wear. Wrangler jeans have that snug Western fit.

WRANGLER WESTERN WEAR is standard

equipment with Bill Linderman and Jim Shoulders, World's 1950 and 1949 All-Around Champs*. Wranglers are Sanforized to keep that "just-right" fit. Jeans have convenient zipper closure that won't warp or buckle—no awkward buttons.

WRANGLERS' rugged 11-oz. denim takes the jolting steer-

wrestling wear of Gerald Roberts and Todd Whatley, World's 1948 and 1947 All-Around Champs. Just try to wear Wranglers out! Jeans for men, $3.69; youths, $3.49; boys, $2.79. Jackets for men, $3.98; shirts, $3.69. Women's jeans (8 oz.), $2.98; girls', $2.79. Money-back guarantee. Blue Bell, Inc., Greensboro, N. C., World's Largest Producer of Work Clothes.

*RCA Ratings

WESTERN JEANS JACKETS AND SHIRTS

BLUE BELL

Wrangler

WRANGLER BLUE BELL 11MW 1947

Wrangler Blue Bells Model 11MW from 1947. MW stands for *Men's Western* and 11MW was the company's first model.
The pants were specially made for people who rode a lot and initially featured arcuate stitch on their back pockets.
But shortly after the launch date, they were sued by Levi's and had to change the design.
In 1948, Wrangler changed it to a big W on each back pocket – an abbreviation for Western Wear.

LEVI'S DELUXE SHIRT 1930

This shirt can be traced through a few different denim collectors all the way back to a man named Don Perry.
Don worked as a cowboy between the late 1930s up to the '60s. The first denim collector bought
the shirt from Perry in Oklahoma, probably giving a good indication as to where he lived.
The garment is from the '30s and quite different to most apparel, keeping in mind that
embroidery would not have a major impact until ten years later.
During this period, Perry purchased rodeo bulls and arranged bull riding events, known
as "Buck's Out", near his own home. Sadly, Don passed away in 2002.

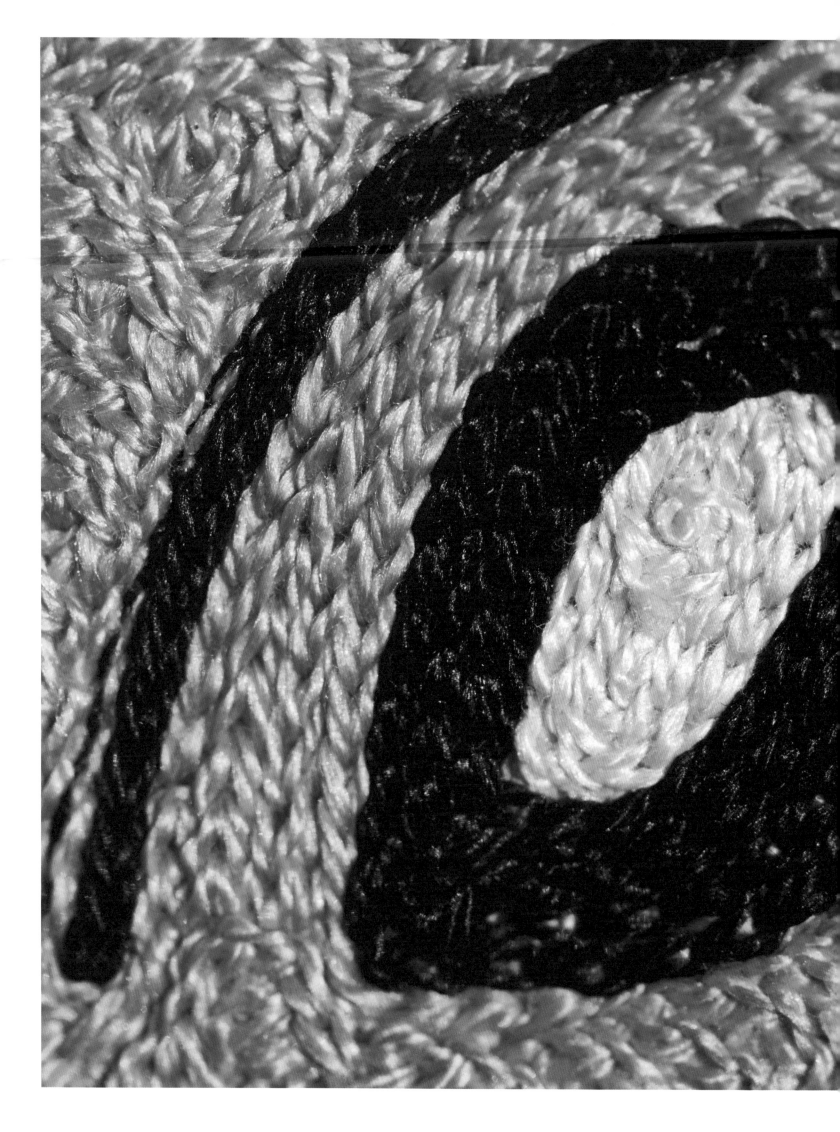

Levi Strauss
DeLuxe
1744
GENUINE LORRAINE
100% WORSTED
FABRIC
DRY CLEAN ONLY

JC PENNEY FOREMOST 1925—35

James Cash Penney came from a simple and humble background. He grew up on a poor farm – something which would come to characterize his personality. Big city life was never really his thing, and he felt most at home in small towns.

James was concerned about the poor quality of milk and meat produced by cattle in the United States. A major cause of this, he argued, was the practice of splitting large cattle herds into smaller groups. So he decided to try to improve the cattle industry and bought a large dairy farm in 1922.

One of his greatest assets was called Langwater Foremost, which was by far the most expensive and most famous bull of the day, costing a whopping twenty thousand dollars. Penney's goal to maximize milk production through maintaining a large (and thereby healthy) heard was met with success. The bull bred some of the most milk-producing cows in history. One of them even broke the world record for milk and butter production.

The bull laid the foundation for the Foremost Dairy Company, a research and training center in agriculture. The bull also lent its name to JC Penney's line of jeans: Foremost.

The pants in the picture are most likely the oldest Foremost jeans.

LEVI'S DENIM FAMILY SHIRT 1954

This shirt belongs to Levi's *Denim Family* and is from the 1950s. It has classic pocket flaps with a "sawtooth design", and snaps.

Jack A. Weil was the man behind the western shirt. He was born in 1901 and got the idea for his innovative shirt design when he saw modern cowboys dressed in leather boots and a cowboy hat, but wearing normal, everyday shirts. Jack wanted to give them a tougher and more handsome image.

He worked up a new design and patented it. His apparel featured the familiar sawtooth pocket flaps and snaps. He also chose fabric that often exhibited strong, bright colors made into distinct patterns.

In 1946, Jack started selling his western shirts through his company Rockmount Ranch Wear. Levi's started making similar shirts with sawtooth pockets first in the '50s, so Jack's patent had most probably expired by then.

Jack is also the inventor of the famous *bolo tie* – a tie made of braided leather straps held together by a decorative buckle. Today, many real and wannabe cowboys wear the popular bolo tie.

Jack's company, located in Denver, Colorado, is still in operation. His grandson Steven Weil manages it, adhering steadfast to his grandfather's inspired words and motto:

"The West is not a place, it is a state of mind."

The trademark "cowboy style" owes Jack – or "Papa Jack" as he was called – a tip of the hat for his enduring influence.

LADY LEVI'S 701 1940

In 1934, Levi's introduced a denim line that was specifically designed for women: the 701, or, "Lady Levi's". The pants were sold only in the western United States before World War II, but after the war, the 701 became a national phenomenon for the simple reason that women did not wear jeans in public in the '30s. But Lady Levi's were daring in another way: they featured a button fly. At this time, using a button fly on women's jeans was highly controversial. But most women actually never liked the buttons, so Levi's modified the 701 and started producing it with zippers in the '40s.

Despite their disputed reputation, 701's were given instant credibility by being featured in fashion magazine Vogue – cementing the model's popularity in the fashion world.

It is common for different jeans brands to have different colored selvedge. Levi's used a white selvedge with a red line. But in Lady Levi's, a pink line was used.

OLD KENTUCKY MFG. CO. 1950

The jacket is an *Old Kentucky* from the 1950s. Starting in 1904, the company had already planted a seed under the name Kentucky Manufacturing Company. Five years later they would switch to the Old Kentucky Manufacturing Co., and start to make all kinds of clothes, including jeans, shirts, jackets, overalls, and more. In 1969, the company re-structured and became the Washington Manufacturing Company, which manufactured the Dee-Cee brand.

H.D. LEE CO. 100J 1968

The Lee Westerner 100J is perhaps one of the most influential denim jackets ever made. It was made with
"westweave", which has a nice, smooth surface, but this doesn't compromise the fabric's strength and durability.
This particular jacket is from 1968, but the model was launched back in 1958. It began when Lee had advertisements
in, among other publications, *Life Magazine*. They used the slogan: "Ranch born. City bred. Lee Westerner."
The jacket was made for more dressed-up occasions and quickly became iconic due to its color, fit and design.

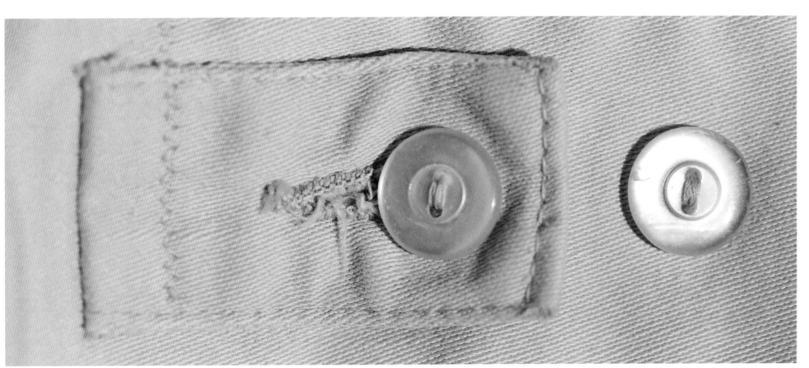

UNION MADE
Lee®
WESTERNER T.M.
SANFORIZED
100-J
40 REGULAR
100% COTTON
MADE IN U.S.A.

H.D. LEE MERCANTILE CO.
101 COWBOY 1926—36

These thirteen ounce heavy pants are from the late 1920s or early '30s. There is a pair of Lee 101's, which were also popularly called "Cowboy Pants". With these jeans, Lee wanted to reach customers who worked as sailors, lumberjacks and of course, cowboys. In other words, people who had physical, hard work which called for durable clothing.

In 1924, production of the 101 started and the heavy, durable pants were immediately met with success. If Levi's flagship model was the 501, so was Lee's counterpart the 101. They are fully on par with each other in terms of success and sales. It wasn't only physical laborers who bought them; rather, their customer base would prove to be much, much larger.

Two years later, Lee launched the 101Z, which were the first jeans with a zipper fly. When the 101Z came out, the 101's started to be called 101B's.

Like many other denim brands, Lee flirted for a while with riveted pockets and made some of its first trousers with rivets – but the company would very soon choose an entirely different method to be used on the back pockets.

Bar tacking was the name of Lee's new solution.

Bar tacking is when a zigzag stitch is sewn very tight to hold together two pieces of fabric. Often the little seam is shaped into a straight line about a centimeter in width. Sometimes the manufacturer sews a cross. In places where Levi's had their metal rivets, Lee instead used a zigzag cross, called a *cross bar tack.*

Bar tacks are one of those innovations that can easily be missed – if you're not looking specifically for them. They are widely used in things such as backpacks, tents, military and police equipment, uniforms of all types, and climbing gear. Some sports apparel has even made bar tacks an integral part of their design. But when it comes to jeans, bar tacks were used especially on pockets, belt loops, the fly, and to enhance the waist and hip.

It is one of those innovations that is so simple, yet so essential. Bar tacks propelled jeans' development forward in a big way. But compared with the cinch back – an innovation each pair of jeans had in its early history – one can easily see that bar tacks have survived the passage of time while the cinch back did not.

There is a strong reason why bar tacks survived: if they were used correctly on a pair of jeans, the small seam could withstand pressure of up to four hundred pounds.

Lee had actually used bar tacks in its overalls back in the 1910s, but the classic *cross bar tack* (x) didn't start to be used until it was applied to the 101.

Quite remarkably, Lee chose not to use rivets – choosing instead a personal and creative way to enhance their jeans which would prove to be very successful. Besides the obvious savings from not using rivets, which required access to expensive copper and riveting machines, Lee's innovation proved there were opportunities to succeed for those companies with the courage to try new things.

With the 101, Lee didn't play it safe, and the design was met with great success.

Nowadays, bar tacks are standard.

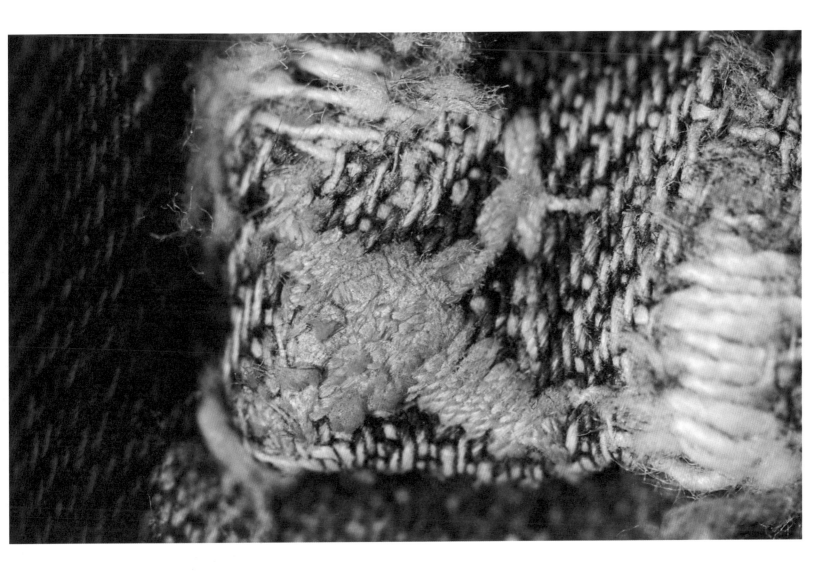

A SAILOR IN JEANS

The smell of oil and hot metal was thick in the air. It was neither day nor night down in the engine room. The only available light was emanating from bulbs that intently watched over the main operating machine. Six large cylinders – a thousand horsepower each – pumped up and down with a relentless rhythm that vibrated through the ship's steel hull, beams, and decks.

Lars-Olof Svedberg kept watch. As one of the more experienced sailors, he was given the midnight to four shift. This was common practice for rookies – daylight was when most of the Vretaholm crew was awake and able to step in if anything happened. But now he was alone, and most of the thirty-five man crew was asleep.

It was hot in the engine room and Lars-Olof wore jeans without a shirt. He was reading an American newspaper. But because they had cast off from Portland, Maine, on the east coast of the U.S. a couple days earlier, the news was no longer current.

It was 1956 and Lars-Olof kept abreast of world events. The Cold War was on, but it would not reach a climax until the '60s. The war in Korea had recently ended. In Cuba, Castro and Guevara were still in the mountains. Their time had not yet arrived to take Havana and overthrow President Batista.

But what characterized the zeitgeist of the '50s the most was optimism and hope for the future. World War II was over. Europe had been rebuilt and the U.S. economy was on top. These were relatively good times.

Lars-Olof was born in Gothenburg and grew up in an area called Majorna, which at that time had the reputation of being a haven for seafarers, shipyard workers, prostitutes, and other lower social classes. His family lived at the top of an old stone house overlooking the entrance to the Port of Gothenburg.

It wasn't just the view of the port that came to shape Lars-Olof's interest in life at sea. His father was an employee at Eriksberg's Shipyard and as a child, Lars-Olof visited there often. He witnessed many peculiar things at the shipyard during World War II, most notably a bullet hole riddled German vessel that was moored for repairs. The many wooden pieces used to plug the hull stuck out like sawed-off bull horns.

Lars-Olof signed up as a sailor and went to sea immediately after finishing secondary school in Gothenburg. His years of waiting were finally over. He was seventeen at the time.

When Lars-Olof enlisted, sailors didn't have strict

relief routines like they do today. Anyone could simply sign up at a Swedish port so long as they understood they might be gone for a long time. Nobody complained about long deployments at sea. It's just how things were done back then. The first thing Lars-Olof learned as a new sailor was the mantra: "Shut up and do the job". This message wasn't intended as a bullying tactic – it was simply part of the job as a sailor.

Lars-Olof recalled an occasion when the main engine broke down. One of the pistons –about two feet in diameter – had loosened. The crew worked for over thirty hours straight – without rest – not because they wanted to, but because they had no choice. At sea, no one was there to come to the rescue. It was important to always be prepared and ready to fix anything that needed repair.

Suddenly, there was noise from the telegraph machine on the bridge. The message was to go on stand-by.

Lars-Olof didn't know for sure what was happening up there, but experience told him that they were probably at risk of a collision.

Then came a second signal.

Full back!

Lars-Olof threw the operating controls into reverse. The ship's fifteen-yard long main engine slowed and started turning the opposite direction amid loud protests.

He looked up, painfully aware that he was four or five yards below the waterline. If a collision occurred, the hull could rupture – putting them all in grave danger.

Viktor sits at his computer and peruses eBay. He opens new pages, scrolls down, and keeps reading. He repeats the process again and again. Methodically. But there are no jeans.

Then his cell phone rings.

It's Viktor's friend and he has seen a pair of old, unused Lee jeans for sale on Tradera, the Swedish equivalent of eBay. The owner is a Swedish man who lives in the country's southernmost region.

Viktor thanks his friend for the tip, but also mentions that it can't be true. Not in Sweden. The chance of vintage jeans becoming available in a small country like Sweden, and *dead stock* at that, was minimal.

But curiosity prevails, and Viktor logs on Tradera's website. He looks up the ad and reads it. His suspicion quickly turns to surprise.

He can hardly believe it's true.

The owner was a sailor in the 1950s and bought the pair of jeans in the U.S. around that time, but he has never used them. Even the price tag is still attached. Dead stock is rare and hard to come by. Finding old vintage garments that are in mint condition and have the price tag intact is extremely rare – especially at a good price.

The jeans are waiting five hundred miles south.

Viktor places his bid.

There was no collision, but the fog was thick and the first mate made the call to reverse as a precaution. Lars-Olof had nothing to worry about.

Up there, above the water, the ship glided gently through the fog and forged slowly forward.

As soon as the sun rose, light cut through the morning haze and chased away the large chunks of gloom still lingering on the water. Once the first officer had gained proper visibility, he ordered the ship full speed ahead. They were bound for Cuba.

Vretaholm's route started in Montréal, Canada, continued south along the east coast of the U.S., and made a few stops on the way to Cuba, including Halifax, Nova Scotia and Portland, Maine. After Havana, they sailed over to Mexico, then north to New Orleans. After stopping in Tampa, Florida, the ship returned back up the coast to Montréal.

A team of dockworkers met the ship's crew in each port. The gang hurried onboard the ship to load and unload. A second gang of workers remained on the dock to take delivery of the goods by cranes. The goods were then loaded on freight trains and trucks, or carried away by wheelbarrow to the warehouses on the quays. When this was finished, the dockworkers continued to unload the freight that would ship out from their own port.

While the dockworkers toiled hour after hour loading and unloading cargo, Lars-Olof and his colleagues put on what they called their "real American" jeans and made the most of their shore leave. On deck, thin cotton pants were usually the work wear used due to the heat emanating from the engine room. But as soon as they landed, they put on their Lee jeans. Some of them meandered off to the harbor bars. Others went shopping.

Lars-Olof did not shop at the big department stores in the center of the cities he visited. He preferred stores catering specifically to sailors and workers – stores that specialized in selling work clothes. He usually got a better price in the specialty stores than at the other places.

He found a good store in every port after some time, but Lee jeans he bought especially in Portland. It wasn't difficult to understand why he preferred that particular store in Portland to the other shops inside the city center. It was a simple, square brick house with an apartment upstairs. Maybe the shopkeeper lived there with his family, it was hard to tell. The curtains were often drawn making it hard to see in.

The whole area was a bustling suburb with decent prices that beckoned Lars-Olof. He could find bargains here.

A striped shade obscured the clothes that hung in the shop windows. There were jeans, jackets, and much more inside. Functionality and quality were prevalent in the store.

A huge sign hung from one corner to the other above the door. The name of the shop was M. Jacobson – Seamen Outfitter & Naval Uniforms.

Lars-Olof often bought several pairs of jeans when he was there. During this era, jeans were not yet available in Sweden. There were a few local businesses that made copies of jeans, but true American jeans were still rare and almost impossible to find. And it was not just Sweden. In the late 1940s and early '50s, jeans were still rare in the rest of Europe too.

Sailors preferred Lee and wore them exclusively. The general consensus was that Lee was the best and a little tougher than the rest, partly because of their leather patches. Sailors also felt that Lee jeans were stronger than the competition. They were simply more durable.

Famous people sometimes came to visit when Vretaholm was in port. Ernest Hemingway himself stood on deck one day, prompting Lars-Olof to hurry down to his two-person cabin and fetch his camera.

This was before televisions were commonplace, so seeing a celebrity was a big deal. Even though there were televisions in the U.S., by the mid-50s, they were still very rare in Sweden. This was also a time when it was very unusual to travel to foreign countries the way Lars-Olof did. One must remember that only twenty years earlier, clipper ships sailed the shipping routes of the seas as the breeze allowed. Times were changing. Wind power had been replaced by large diesel engines.

The world was quickly becoming more accessible.

But life at sea was basically the same then as it is now.

It was characterized by good friendships, hard work, and vulnerability. The attitude throughout the ages was that a sailor kept quiet and carried on.

On Vretaholm, the crew worked in four-hour shifts, which were followed by eight hours of rest before the next shift. They worked like this round the clock, week after week. Sleep patterns at sea were indeed quite unusual.

Still, no one would ever think to complain.

The foundation for how the jeans of today look was laid back in the 1950s. The design and the profile of jeans from that era have stayed with the garment ever since.

Another advent of the '50s was that jeans were marketed directly to children and adolescents for the first time. Lee had a special model of children's jeans with an extra leather patch on the back of one pocket. It was called *pen burn* and did not have a brand name on the label. The idea was the owner could burn his name on the label – or a scout number if the child was a member of the Boy or Girl Scouts.

Lee's retailers had the equipment required to do this and marketed it with the slogan:

"Just tell your Lee dealer to burn it in!"

After an almost two year absence, Lars-Olof was back in Sweden again. He stepped ashore and felt the ground rolling beneath him, not used to stepping on anything solid for some time.

He said goodbye to his friends and left the harbor.

Last time he had been home in Sweden, he met a girl named Monica. He longed for her and had already decided that his time at sea was over. Life abroad couldn't be reconciled with family life, and he and Monica wanted to get married and have children. He knew he would not regret it.

Lars-Olof threw his seaman's bag over his shoulder. In it lay the perfect gift.

A pair of "real Americans".

Viktor won the bidding and was soon in contact with Lars-Olof.

It's a dark February night when Viktor parks his car in Staffanstorp. The five hundred mile journey is finally over. Now he's here, in the south of Sweden: Skåne. Specifically, Viktor finds himself in a residential area where the houses are built closely together in independent rows. Manicured lawns and shrubbery line the walkways. One by one, leafless birch trees throw a patchwork of shadows across the asphalt. The neighborhood peacefully rests.

Viktor soon locates the right house. He has barely opened the tall gate that leads into an intimate garden when he sees Lars-Olof welcoming him from the front door.

The tall, handsome man in his seventies greets Viktor. Physically fit, his hair is white and his beard neatly trimmed. The first two buttons of his white shirt are unbuttoned and he wears dark beige chinos. Lars-Olof's whole persona conveys confidence. He displays a warm – and at the same time awake – look.

Viktor also has the opportunity to meet his wife Monica, now a retired deacon. An intelligent and sweet

△ THIS PICTURE WAS TAKEN in the 1950s. Lars-Olof stands on deck, taking a breath of fresh air. His shift in the engine room will begin soon.
Waiting for him in every nook and corner downstairs is the smell of hot metal and oil.
Behind him stretches the Saint Lawrence River. Once again the ship leaves Montréal behind, with new cargo in its holds.

woman, she is seated at her computer sorting through family photos when Viktor arrives. The finished album is a gift for the couple's children and grandchildren.

She quickly puts out some coffee and cinnamon buns bought from the grocery store. The new friends talk while they enjoy the coffee.

Viktor listens to Lars-Olof's story about how he purchased the jeans in the U.S. in the 1950s and how they went unused. Lars-Olof jokingly says the reason is because he doesn't think he could fit in them anymore. He often bought several pairs simultaneously for either his own use or to give away as gifts. But for some reason, this pair of Lees had remained unworn. Even the price tag is still attached.

Lately, Lars-Olof is occupied with what he – in a somewhat macabre way – calls "death cleaning". It's when you do away with and sell your prized possessions – before any knowledge of their value is lost.

The pair of Lee's he's selling to Viktor is one such article. He bought them in 1956 for five dollars and ninety-five cents, which at that time corresponded to about thirty Swedish crowns. But now, as dead stock, the jeans are obviously worth much more. Lars-Olof is intent on selling his prized possessions to people who will really appreciate them. He's not certain if his descendants would have a sense for the cultural significance of these jeans – maybe they would throw them out or simply use them as a normal pair of pants. No, Lars-Olof is intent on ensuring the jeans' legacy lives on. That is what he and Viktor have in common.

History is worth preserving.

Viktor backs out from a parking space and begins the long drive home. Meanwhile, he thinks of what Lars-Olof told him as they stood in the doorway saying goodbye.

"In the 1950s, people looked back at the end of the 1800's with a sense that it was the Stone Age. A lot had happened since then."

Viktor drives onto the highway and accelerates. He is happy. On the seat next to him is the latest addition to his collection: yet another pair of unique vintage jeans. And with them he's not only received an anecdote, but an entire life story.

"The '50s are perhaps the Stone Age for you today", Lars-Olof continued. "I don't know. But it wasn't for me who lived it."

▽ FROM TIME TO TIME visitors would come onboard when Vretaholm was docked at port. On this particular day, it was Ernest Hemingway himself who was offered a tour of the ship. Lars-Olof is behind the lens, out of breath after running below deck to search for his camera.

△ THE SHIP *Vretaholm's* route.

LARS-OLOF STANDING IN FRONT of his favorite store in Portland, Maine, where he often shopped for jeans. It was here where he found the pair of Lee Riders 101Z's that he sold decades later to Viktor.

LARS-OLOF ON WATCH down in the engine room, wearing Lee jeans, or "real Americans" as the sailors of Vretaholm used to call them.

H.D. LEE CO. 101Z 1952

Lee Riders 101Z's appeared in the early '50s and had a U-shaped crotch for better comfort.
The pants were a clear example of H. D. Lee Company's shifted focus from only manufacturing
work clothes to creating everyday clothes that appealed to the masses.
"Lazy S" stitching on the back pockets – what Lee is known for today – debuted in 1944.
The idea was that together, the two slightly curved seams mimic the horns of the famous
Longhorn cattle in the western United States.
The jeans in the pictures are from 1952, and were probably from the very first
production run of Lee Riders 101Z's.

H.D. LEE CO. "PEN BURN" 1946

The H. D. Lee Company did not just make jeans for cowboys and seasoned sailors, but had many other innovative ideas as well. *Pen burn* was one of these. On the back of these jeans is an extra leather patch where the owner could burn his or her name or troop number (if involved in a scouting troop). It became popular among children in the '50s, and made it easier for busy parents to distinguish which pants belonged to whom. These specific pants are from 1946.

"I AM THE JOPLIN OVERALL GIRL"

Compliments of the Joplin Overall Co.

Joplin, Mo.

AN UNDERDOG'S REVENGE

Today, everyone from programmers, teachers, farmers, and cleaners wears jeans. Even politicians wear them. People wear them at work and for play. Denim has managed to permeate all levels of society, but it's easy to forget this wasn't always the case.

Most people have a certain relationship with jeans. Regardless of what anyone thinks about the garment, jeans always evoke an emotion.

It can certainly be said today that jeans are regarded with more acceptance and respect than they were in the 1950s and before. At that time, denim was still a symbol of the working class poor and the have-nots. The general attitude until the '50s was that it was unacceptable to wear jeans at places like restaurants, theaters, cinemas or at other social events. Jeans were associated with physical labor and their status was therefore low. People didn't wear jeans daily back then like they do today. Sure, there were some people back in the 1930s and '40s who frequently wore jeans, but these folks were mostly artists, musicians, writers, and certain intellectuals with left-wing bents – in other words: people who lived outside the norm of society because of their professions or political ideals. Maybe this was the reason denim became something of a

rebel symbol when the '50s started?

Hollywood soon changed the popular mindset associated with jeans. Young, good-looking men were dressed in jeans, t-shirts, and leather jackets in popular films. They were the new kind of anti-heroes who stood up against the establishment. The youth recognized themselves in them and took to wearing jeans with open arms.

The 1950s would be "the decade of the teen". Adolescence wasn't regarded as a special period in a person's life prior to this time. Before the '50s, one was either a child or an adult. Children went to school and started working at an early age. But during the 1900s, as the amount of schooling increased and secondary schools became commonplace, a teenage culture was born. This concept would crystallize as the decades passed and the term teenager was coined sometime in the '50s.

Adults did not approve of children and young people imitating their favorite actor's dress and style, often believing Hollywood celebrities were bad role models. Neat and tidy school uniforms were the accepted form of youth dress and adults were particularly horrified when young people started wearing jeans to school. Opposition to denim culture was greatest on the East Coast of the U.S. where people were worried their children would rebel against all types of authority if they dressed in jeans. Some schools even decided to take a hard line against these "problem kids" and prohibited the wearing of denim during school hours.

Of course, bans like this often experience the opposite of the intended effect when it comes to children and young people. The denim bans were no different. They just made jeans more desirable for young people and sales surged at stores that sold jeans.

Jeans companies were quick to capitalize on young people's interest in their products. They started campaigning in the late 1950s to get denim accepted in schools, not just for "problem kids", but for every type of kid. Levi's had advertisements that read: "Denim: Right for School."

Society at large was moving towards freer fashion at this time. This was especially true with jeans, which came to be regarded not just as work clothes, but clothes that could be used in everyday life. Manufacturers realized where the big money was and developed special models for certain demographics. For example, Lee started making their *Double Knees* in 1957. These were a pair of jeans specifically designed for boys who often wore out the knees in their denim. Additionally, Erwin Mills of Durham, North Carolina, started selling jeans with the slogan: "Clean Jeans for Teens."

In 1954, Levi's launched a family collection called *The Denim Family*. This was yet another example that jeans were crossing over from work wear to casual wear.

Still, there were those who had difficulty accepting jeans. Many people felt that denim was something crass and those who wore it had no style.

African Americans didn't dress in denim during this time either – but for an entirely different reason. Jeans reminded them of the South, slavery, and the work that was done in the fields. But even this sentiment would eventually fade and change.

Slowly, society's attitude towards jeans improved and resistance loosened. School principals came to realize that the denim bans were useless and did away with them. People started going to movies and restaurants dressed in denim. Denim garments slowly gained ground.

One might argue that the restrictions on jeans helped increase their popularity and eventually led to their acceptance in society at large. Denim was seemingly a misunderstood rebel that grew to be accepted over time.

Years passed and many jeans companies began to establish themselves internationally. They found new markets.

The 1960s were largely a decade of change. The Berlin Wall went up in 1961, and a year after that, the Cuban missile crisis threatened to start World War III. Two important men, John F. Kennedy and Martin Luther King, were both assassinated. In August '69, Woodstock became the world's most visited festival. It was the hippie era and many young people protested against the Vietnam War. Many of them took a step outside of normal society – opting to live in collectives out in nature and far from society's rules, norms and obligations. There, they nurtured an open view of nudity, ate vegetarian fare, and lived in an environmentally friendly way. Young people of this time rebelled against their parents' generation, which they believed thought and acted wrong. Jeans became the uniform of the 1960s youth.

Earlier in the '50s, people embroidered their jeans to show who they were or where they came from. It's interesting to think that, while the youth were against uniforms and the uniformity of society, they used embroidery as a way to promote camaraderie and display their affiliation with a certain club or gang. It could be a far-fetched thought, but perhaps this use of embroidery made jeans a type of uniform unto itself. One could argue that during the '60s and '70s, jeans became a symbol of young people's political values and their rebellion against the status quo.

Viktor is packing up a box in the kitchen of his new apartment. Recently, he has been worried that something will happen to his collection. He's not so worried about theft, but rather that it could be destroyed in a fire.

The museum curator really hit a nerve. During her short visit to Stockholm, she told Viktor that his Levi's N° 2's from 1888-89 would be insured as long as they were on loan to the museum in Rotterdam. She told him he had nothing to worry about.

But still.

Two years ago, Viktor's friend Mike took steps to protect his collection and moved it to a safe location. After Mike published his book, *Jeans of the Old West: A History*, he was nervous that someone would break into his house and steal his collection.

Viktor's cell phone rings. He stops what he's doing

and answers. It's an insurance company. They have discovered he doesn't have home insurance and want to discuss options with him.

Viktor tells them about his denim collection and the piece he treasures most: the old N° 2's. He says he has been thinking about insuring them for a long time. The woman on the phone says he must first and foremost take pictures of everything in his collection.

Viktor wonders if it's really worth it. It might be too much work and take too long.

There have been several experiments with denim over the years. Chambray and Jelt are two examples previously mentioned. The changes made to denim were probably implemented to make it more comfortable to wear. One such attempt was Wrangler's model *13MWZ*, launched by the company in 1964. It was made with a new innovation called *broken twill*.

Denim is made of tightly woven cotton threads of two different varieties. "Warp" are the white threads that make up the width of the fabric and "weft" are the threads that are dyed with indigo. The warp and weft threads are woven diagonally against each other, either in one direction or the other. This creates diagonal lines in the fabric called *twill weave*. The two different variants are called *right hand twill* (also called *z twill*), and *left hand twill* (or *s twill*).

Levi's became famous because of their "right hand". It was – and still is – their standard. It is also the most common weave today.

"Left hand" was originally used by Lee. It wears down more smoothly than "right hand" and ends up feeling softer against the hand after being washed.

Broken twill, on the other hand, weaves right and left in the fabric so that a zigzag pattern is formed. This twill is durable, comfortable to wear, and has a natural stretch, even if it's made entirely of cotton. Moreover, it doesn't look like either right or left twill weave. The surface has no visible graininess like the other two. Broken twill wears differently too. Therefore, it has a distinctive and unique look.

Perhaps the biggest advantage of broken twill is that it counteracts the typical twisting that occurs when washing regular denim. This is when the pant leg twists to one side so that the seam on that side also twists forward. Twisting was a common trait of the jeans of yesteryear, but it has been resolved in today's jeans.

During the 1960s, pre-shrunk, or sanforized denim, had a great impact and became the industry standard.

Jeans had a place in every man's wardrobe and became widely accepted by the late '60s. This fact was evidenced by the chain stores in the U.S. that began to manufacture jeans. The J.C. Penney chain had several popular lines in the '60s and '70s, including the *Big Mac, Foremost,* and *Ranch Craft*. However, they had already been making jeans for a long time. Initially, J.C. Penney's jeans were straight copies of Levi's. Big Mac, the mark they launched in 1922, is the company's oldest brand of work clothing still sold today.

James Cash Penney – the man behind the J.C. Penney Company – was the head of one of America's largest department store chains. At its peak, it totaled twelve hundred stores in all fifty states, plus Mexico, Chile, and Puerto Rico. But Penney's start was far from successful. He was the son of a poor farmer, and grew up on a farm near Hamilton, Missouri. He had eleven siblings, of whom he was number seven. His religious parents had a good relationship with them and infused them with solid values and morals. Among other lessons, they encouraged James to buy his own clothes when he was eight years old to teach him the value of money. This was also due to the family's lack of money. Penney raised livestock for a time in order to make money, but had to quit after neighbors complained about the smell.

He worked on the family farm after high school, but his father died a short time later. Before his father passed away, he arranged a job for Penney in a clothing store. Within little time, he passed a course in salesmanship and went to work for several different stores by the close of the 1800s.

In 1902, Penney opened his first namesake store. He and his family lived in the attic upstairs. Penney operated his first store in the same manner that he would later manage the entire J. C. Penney chain. He bought only high quality goods and sold them at an inexpensive price. But above all, he built the chain based on well-trained, loyal, and hardworking employees – employees who knew how to give good service to customers. James prioritized good employees. It was the employees who made the heart and soul of the company.

He opened two new stores within the first year and continued to expand his business at a feverish pace. By 1924, Penney opened his five hundredth store. He died in 1971 at ninety-five years old, but the department store chain survived.

J.C. Penney advertised their jeans by contrasting them against other well-known brands: "The big difference between us and them is the back pocket. And the price." By removing, among other things, the slick arcuate stitch on the back pockets, they could charge just ten dollars for their jeans – something their advertising prominently featured: "Fancy stitching - fancy price tag."

Marilyn Monroe wore J.C. Penney pants. She even wore a pair in one of her films.

Jeans were mostly a male phenomenon until the 1960s. As a specific working garment, they were most predominately used in male-dominated professions. They were miners, lumberjacks, sailors and train workers. Mechanics, electricians, and plumbers. These were the types of jobs men did during the time.

But there were exceptions. In 1908, denim dungarees for women were produced for the first time. Women who worked in factories during the First and Second World Wars wore clothing made from denim. However, jeans were not a standard garment made for women until the '60s. If women wore jeans before this time, they were probably jeans made for men.

The reason for this late acceptance of jeans among women likely had to do with something more significant than the fit. Maybe the early attempts at "women's jeans", such as Levi's Freedom-Alls, or Lady Levi's from the '30s, were simply ahead of their time? Maybe society was simply not ready to see women in jeans?

Historically, the combination of women and jeans has always been a sensitive one. In 1600s England, women who wore men's clothing could face the death penalty. There is thankfully no death penalty for wearing improper attire today, but women who wear trousers still experience resistance and prejudice in some cultural backwaters.

The popular perception of women and jeans all changed in the 1960s when denim companies began mass-producing jeans for women. Previously, the zipper had been on one side of the trousers, but now it was moved to the front. An interesting side note is that the button fly has never been used on women's jeans. Of course, the most important adaptation was that jeans were finally manufactured to fit women's bodies. They sat better, were more comfortable, and definitely looked better.

The popularity of jeans rose throughout the world when women in Western countries began wearing them. Now the other half of humanity was taking part in the jeans market, and as such, sales increased significantly. Perhaps the most important turning point was in the 1970s when well-known designers such as Ralph Lauren and Giorgio Armani began producing jeans for women. They also designed jackets, shirts, dresses, skirts, dungarees and overalls. Denim suddenly became glamorous and hip. This naturally affected the price, and the cost of jeans sky-rocketed from a few dollars to hundreds of dollars for a pair of authentic designer jeans.

Then an interesting thing happened: when a new pair of jeans cost as much as a pair of dress trousers, fancy restaurants and hotels no longer had a good argument for denying a man entry for dressing in denim.

Designers in the '70s brought about the notion that it was very important to show what kind of brand was being worn – especially in status-seeking circles. The small label sewn on the back pocket showed others the affluence of the wearer. Wearing a brand became a marker of how much a person cared about his or her own image, and was a factor in whether he or she was "inside" or "outside" a particular group or trend. This was quite unlike the 1800s when a worker simply entered a shop asking for a pair of jeans and took the pants that were handed to him. Most often, the workers didn't even try the jeans on in the store because it was not considered "manly". Quality was the deciding factor of their purchases at the time, not the brand. But that was a different era.

In 1936, Levi's introduced the little *red tab*, which has been mentioned previously. Levi's wrote their name on it in capital letters as: "LEVI'S." Today, collectors call this insignia the *Big E*. In 1971, they switched to a small 'e' in the *batwing* design because it matched better with a real name – in this case, the founder's name. However, it took some years before the change found its place in the small, red mark.

Levi's even tried having a red cloth patch without any brand name, which made it virtually an empty "tab". According to Levi's, they have used this unique tab design for the last thirty-odd years and continue to do so. The reason that Levi's used – and still uses – an empty label was to strengthen the rights of the company's brand on its tabs. In the United States today, only Levi Strauss & Co. has the right to use a tab on their clothing. Having an empty patch reinforces this style of use.

Either way, brand identity has been extremely important for both businesses and consumers since the '60s and '70s.

The old Blue Bell jeans lie on the floor and Viktor looks at the display of his cell phone as he moves it closer to the rivets and arcuate stitch on one of the back pockets. He then takes a picture. This is one of many, many pictures he has taken over the last few days.

If anyone is to thank for this, it must be the woman from the insurance company. She was the one who gave Viktor the idea to photograph his jeans collection, but it has taken a while for him to make it a habit.

The doorbell rings and Viktor welcomes in a friend

who has stopped by with his new camera. The friend is an amateur photographer, and promised to take pictures of Viktor's denim collection. He also needs to practice with his new camera.

An hour passes and the photo shoot is in full swing. They have no idea what the outcome will be, but they have a structured approach and shoot Viktor's material era by era and detail by detail.

In short order, Viktor comes up with the idea of starting a portfolio of his jeans. He wants to compile one so he can use it while traveling. He would be able to show others what he has, and also use the pictures for informational and educational purposes. Of course, Viktor wants to make the best-looking, coolest portfolio ever. It's an all-or-nothing approach, so he makes an appointment with a friend who works at a printing company.

But the price for publishing the portfolio gives Viktor sticker shock. It's just too much money – especially for something that he did not intend to sell. The size of the project has grown as the collection has been photographed and has become something more than an archive of pictures for insurance sake. Viktor decides that he wants to use the thousands of photographs he and his friend now possess for something else – something that feels more meaningful and better manages the rich history and heritage of his jeans.

The history of jeans is really the story of an underdog that made it all the way from the dirtiest and most miserable working environments – where cholera and typhoid took the lives of miners in the late 1800s – to the cat walks of the world's major fashion centers by the 1970s. Of course, the popularity of jeans continues today with an explosion of new denim brands and continuously rising sales figures. It's a story of vindication considering the belittlement and banning of jeans during the '50s, followed by the increased acceptance of the '60s and fashion forward leap in the '70s. Denim has become stylish, respected and conventional. Frankly, it has been a way of life for many. And while denim has always made for a practical and durable garment, the way jeans have been used has changed over the years, leading to the fabric wearing out in completely different ways.

It's a well-known fact that women buy more clothes than men, and perhaps always have. Is it then reasonable to assume that increased jeans sales led the designers of the '70s to seize the great profit potential of making women's jeans – or could the opposite be true? Did designer jeans themselves increase the market size and subsequent sales and profits? Maybe it doesn't matter which scenario was the catalyst in this case because the fact remains:

With designer jeans and their associated high prices denim's status in society was elevated.

With that said, one might wonder if the huge popularity and acceptance of jeans in the world has to do with something besides teenagers simply dressing like their favorite actors – a notion that seems to be the prevailing view.

Instead, might this big breakthrough primarily have been caused by women beginning to wear jeans?

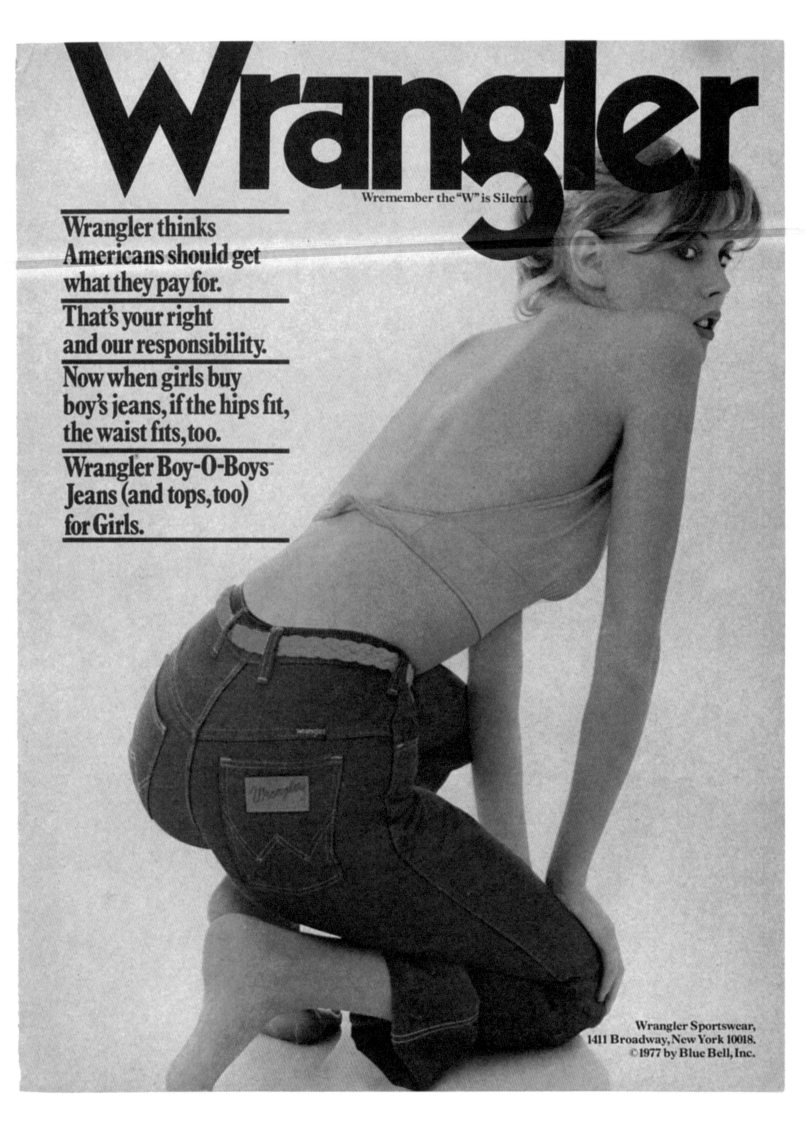

Wrangler

Wremember the "W" is Silent.

Wrangler thinks Americans should get what they pay for.

That's your right and our responsibility.

Now when girls buy boy's jeans, if the hips fit, the waist fits, too.

Wrangler Boy-O-Boys™ Jeans (and tops, too) for Girls.

△ TIMES WERE CHANGING and jeans were no longer exclusive to men. They started to be produced in women's models and styles, and designed specifically for the female body. Now it was possible for women to wear denim pants in public, something that had not previously been popular or very widely accepted.

LEVI'S 705 1969–71

From the text on the back and embroidery on the front, one can deduce that the jacket probably belonged to a student at the University of Texas at El Paso (UTEP). The university was founded in 1914 as The Texas State School of Mines and Metallurgy. The College of Mines and Metallurgy is part of the university. In 1967, the school was given its current name.

Above the front left breast pocket, three Greek letters are embroidered: Alpha, Phi, and Omega. They were the Greek letters for a male fraternity of engineering and geology students, abbreviated APO. The fraternity was founded in 1919. Today, Alpha Phi Omega National Service Fraternity has more than seventeen thousand members of both sexes in the United States.

Taking all this into consideration, it becomes very clear that each garment has its own, unique story to tell.

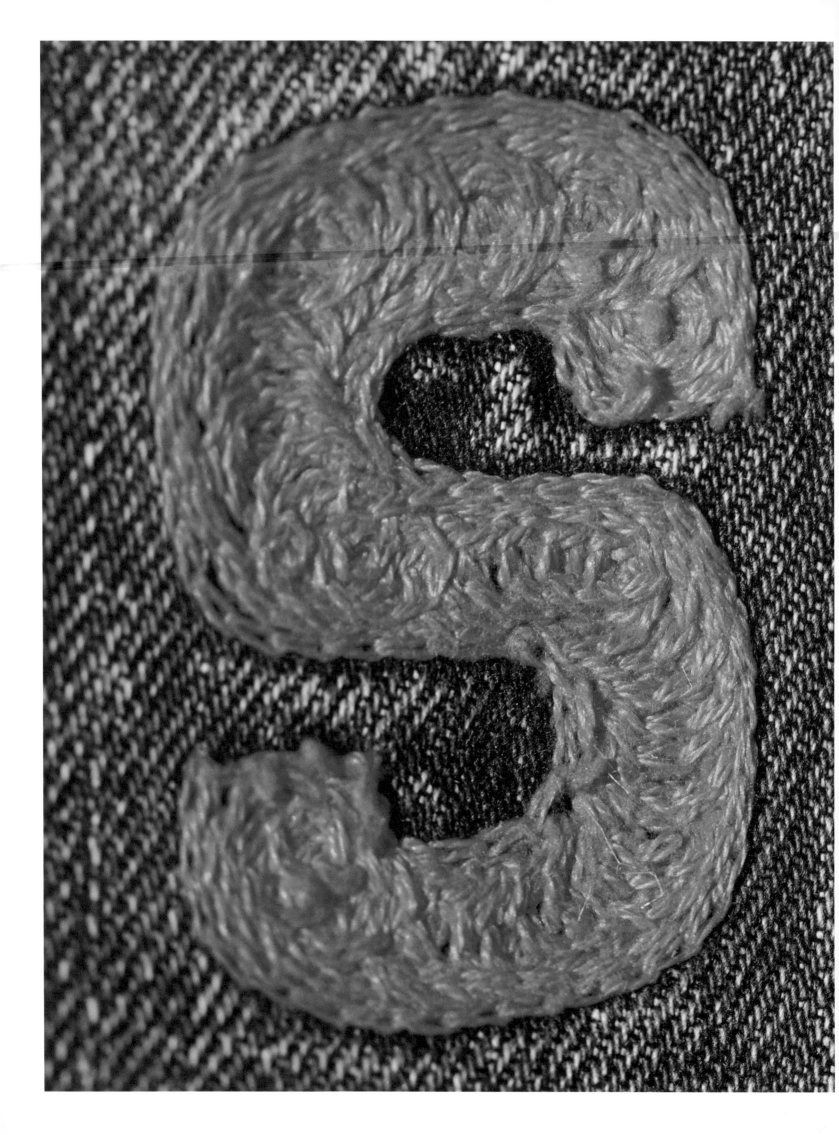

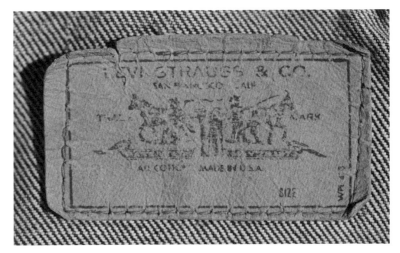

JC PENNEY RANCHCRAFT 1970

Pants from the late '60s to early '70s.

The big difference between us and them is the pocket.

And the price.

The jeans with the fancy stitching on the back are the world's best-selling jeans. Fancy stitching—fancy price tag. The jeans on the right are JCPenney Plain Pockets. They cost $10.00. Which would you rather have? A half-cent's worth of stitching on your pocket, or some extra money in your pocket. Available in denim and new Denim Extra.

Plain Pockets Jeans
only at
JCPenney

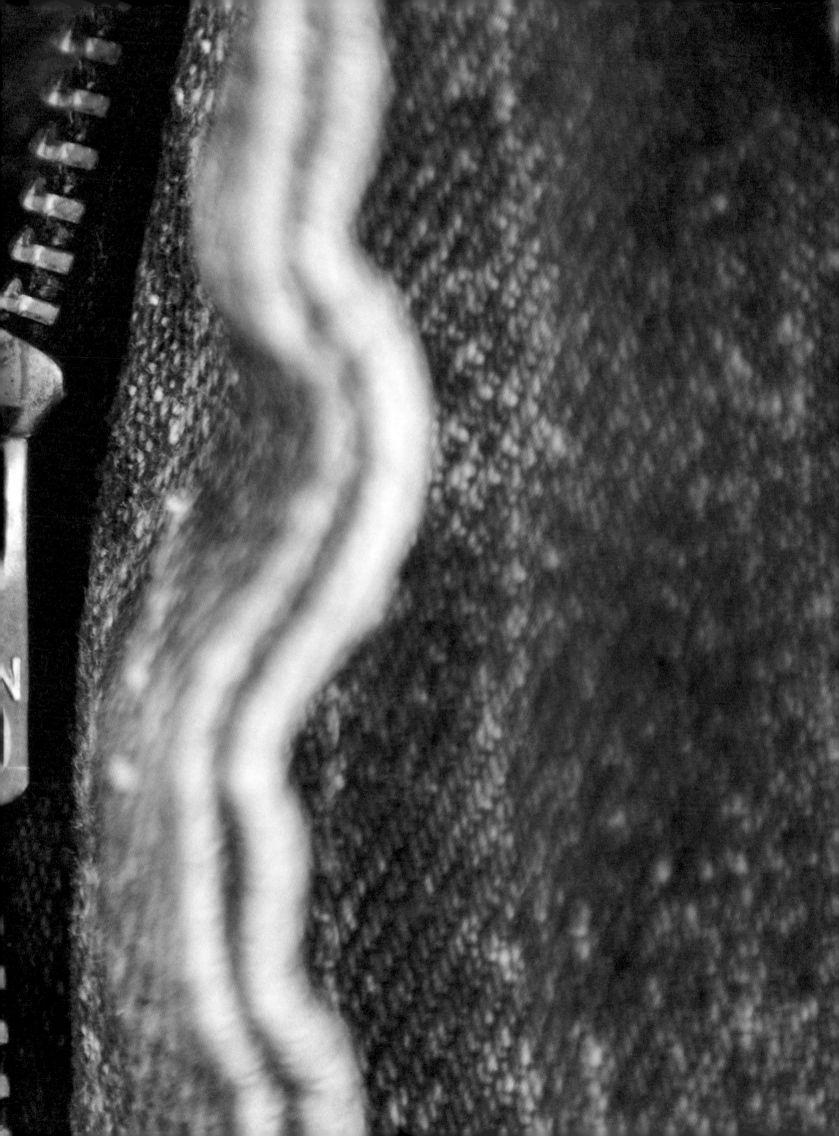

△ PROOF THAT JEANS began to be accepted in society came when school children were allowed to wear them during school hours, which was strictly forbidden before. The picture is most probably from the '50s or '60s, when rules regarding to jeans began to relax.

Like 'em? You'll love 'em!
For value, looks, wear

Oshkosh B'gosh
BRONKS

Smart cowboy styling, husky Sanforized denim, shrinkage less than 1%. Super-reinforced with scratch-proof copper rivets; strong stitching that will *outwear the pants*. Buy BRONKS your size— they never shrink!

- **HIS** rugged 11-ounce Western denim. Zipper fly. Sizes 27 to 36 waist.
- **HERS** styled like *his* but cut for *you* with zipper fly front for extra smooth over-hip fit. Strong 8-ounce Western denim. Sizes 23 to 32 waist.
- **TOTS** just like big brother's or sister's. Same sturdy denim, long wear, neat fit. Ages 1 to 12.

BRONKS, men's, boys', women's, girls', are a specialty of Oshkosh B'Gosh, famous for over a half century as makers of
"The World's Best Work Wear"
At your Oshkosh B'Gosh dealer's, or write

Oshkosh B'gosh Inc. OSHKOSH, WISCONSIN

LEVI'S 559 1962—68

DIFFERENT SHADES OF BLUE

*When people hear the word **jeans**, they often conjure up an image of **blue jeans**. That's because the garment has been traditionally dyed blue since the very beginning. Other colors were not used for jeans until well into the 1900s.*

But why blue and not another color?

Blue is a naturally useful color for clothing. Blue is light enough that it doesn't get too hot in a sunny and warm climate, but not so bright that it easily shows dirt and sweat deposits. Blue also appeals to the eye.

Blue is the third basic color and many people's favorite color. It is often described as peaceful, orderly and safe, and in many cultures symbolizes reliability, intelligence, truth, and sky.

Indigo, a deeper blue, symbolizes personal insight and a deep understanding of things. It is a symbol of wisdom and self-control.

Perhaps blue was picked as the choice color for denim because of these positive associations. However, the most likely reason was due to the availability of indigo dye. The indigo plant has played an important role over the centuries, and not only in its use as a dye.

A framed photo hangs on the wall. In it, three well-dressed men stand next to a woman seated in an armchair. She is wearing an old-fashioned dress. The figures look straight at the camera through a cloud of thin smoke that rises up from the sides. They are all wearing clown makeup.

Viktor looks around. He is in a photography studio that his friend rents along with a few other photographers. One of them is Fredrik, a professional photographer. He is also the one responsible for the clown picture hanging on the wall. There are more photos here too. The walls are full of them.

Viktor and Fredrik hit it off immediately and start talking about Viktor's project. Fredrik is excited about the concept and wonders if he can take pictures of models wearing Viktor's jeans. It's a wonderful idea and Viktor doesn't hesitate to give his approval.

The photo shoot is underway a short time later. Viktor and Fredrik head to an old rail yard with a few models and photograph them next to the trains. They don't have plans for a final product at this point, but the shoot proves fruitful as they capture photos of the denim-clad models based on the periods and original environments of Viktor's jeans.

The results are so good that Viktor and Fredrick discuss doing something special with the photos.

In the beginning, true indigo was used to dye denim. Indigo is a dye derived from the plant kingdom. It can be extracted from several different kinds of plants, but the most natural variety is found in a species named *Indigofera*, which grows in the tropics. Subvarieties Indigofera *tinctoria* and Indigofera *suffruticosa* are the most used of the species.

Indigofera tinctoria is also called "true indigo". It is a shrub that grows between three and six feet high. Depending on the climate, the age of the indigo plant might vary from one-year to several years old. It is a legume with light green, feather-like leaves that grow on each side of a common branch exhibiting tufts of pink or violet flowers.

Many Asian countries, such as India, China and Japan, have used indigo for centuries, especially for coloring silk. Even earlier, indigo was used by the ancient civilizations of Mesopotamia and Egypt, and in the Roman Empire and Ancient Greece. It is a crop with a long and checkered history. During the 1700s and 1800s, indigo was linked to slavery in America, and was one of the most important crops of the time.

Indigo is one of the oldest dyes used to stain clothes and printed materials. It was used on the Arabian Peninsula and in sub-Saharan Africa as face and body paint during festivities. In the same areas, indigo was also used for tattoos because it had a reputation for being antiseptic and was considered protection against evil forces. According to archaeological findings, indigo was used in Egypt in this way as early as 3000 BC. But indigo has other applications. For example, clothing that is dyed with natural indigo acts as a deterrent against blood-sucking insects that spread disease.

Indigo has been used extensively in medical contexts. Chinese research in the 1980s showed that indigo extract was used effectively to treat ailments like eye diseases, jaundice, and meningitis. Its variety of uses is many.

Extracting color from the indigo plant is a complex and time-consuming process, which is accomplished using almost the same methods throughout the world. Since the blue dye is not mature in the plant, the petals are soaked in water so that they ferment. Approximately twelve hours later, the water begins to foam, which is the sign that fermentation has started. After three to five hours in the cold water, the bubbles change color from white to purple. The water, which is now slightly greenish yellow, is then discarded.

The next stage is called *whisking*. In India, for example, people from a special low caste are responsible for the whisking. The fermented indigo petals are kept in buckets and moved around by hand if a relatively small amount is to be whisked. If it is a large-scale production, Indian workers stand in a shallow basin of thigh-high water while kicking back with their legs to whip up oxygen in the dye bath. Regardless of the scale of production, it's hard work.

The dye oxidizes and becomes indigo blue, or *indigotin*, when it is whisked, after which it clumps and sinks to the bottom. The dye bath is first green and then turns dark blue. The art in the process is knowing when the dye bath is ready. At the opportune time, the water is drained out and the paint clumps are collected, dried, and pressed into large cakes of indigo color. It takes roughly one kilo of leaves to produce two to three grams of dried indigo color.

People long sought to create indigo artificially because genuine indigo dye is laborious and difficult to produce. Synthetic indigo was finally invented in the late 1800s, which inevitably made it less expensive to color things like jeans. However, it was not until 1897 that "Indigo Pure" came to market. Indigo Pure immediately overtook sales of real indigo. The price was about the same as the original, but it lacked genuine indigo's inherent medicinal properties and effects against insects. The biggest advantages of artificial indigo color was that it was constant, consistent, and standardized. A few years later, the price of Indigo Pure was cut in half.

An interesting historical fact from World War I is that English and French army uniforms were stained with authentic indigo from their colonies while the Germans used synthetic indigo. The outlook for the synthetic indigo industry looked pale during the mid 1900s, but it was rescued after World War II by the explosion of blue jeans. In the United States today, ninety-eight percent of all synthetic indigo is used to dye denim. The rest is used as food coloring.

Most of the indigo produced today is consumed by the textile industry. Perhaps the biggest fabric manufacturer of the past was the Columbia, South Carolina based Olympian Cotton Mills. They had twelve thousand four hundred looms operating and one hundred and four thousand spindles which spun cotton yarns.

Another textile manufacturer was Swift Denim, founded in 1886. It was a conglomerate of companies located in the cotton districts in southern USA. During the mid-1900s, Swift made the denim used by both Lee and Levi's.

Burlington Industries was another major force in textiles. Burlington began production in 1923 in Burlington, NC, and later moved to Greensboro, North Carolina – the same city as the oldest denim producer that still is in operation today: Cone Denim.

Today Cone Denim and Burlington operate as part of the same parent company, International Textile Group.

The Cones were Jewish immigrants from Bavaria in Germany. The family consisted of Herman Kahn, and his sister and her family. Herman changed his surname from Kahn to Cone when he immigrated in order to make it sound more American. Herman and his brother-in-law, Jacob Adler, opened a merchandising store in Jonesboro, Tennessee, and sold fabrics, clothes, shoes, and even food. They differentiated themselves from stores with similar goods by selling ready-made clothes and not just fabric by the meter. This was an uncommon practice in the southern U.S. at the time.

During the Civil War, Herman and Jacob closed the store and instead put their money into real estate. But as soon as the war was over, they resumed business under the new name Adler, Cone, and Shipley.

Herman and his wife had two sons, Moses and Ceasar, who would later start the Proximity Manufacturing Company – the original name for the Cone Mills Company.

Moses and Ceasar bought the C. E. Graham Mill Manufacturing Company located in Asheville, North Carolina, and produced cotton fabrics. Slow sales made the Cone brothers realize that the Southern mills really needed someone to sell their fabrics. In 1891 the brothers formed Cone Export and Commission Company. The new company represented thirty eight Southern textile mills to sell and market their products worldwide.

After another few years, Moses and Ceasar built a textile factory in Greensboro that they named Proximity Cotton Mills. This new plant was used specifically for denim production. Shortly thereafter, the two brothers built another denim factory, White Oak Mills. The first fabric rolled off the looms in the spring of 1905. Three years later, White Oak was the world's largest denim producer.

Besides denim, the Cone Mills Corporation manufactured corduroy, flannel, and cotton fabrics for most of the 1900s. The actual name "Cone Mills Corporation" was used until shortly after World War II.

In the early 1900s, the company built five small villages around its factories in Greensboro. These villages were named after the factories that the employees worked in: Proximity, Revolution, White Oak, East White Oak, and Print Works. The Cone Mills Company positioned itself to take care of its workers' every need – a strategy that also helped keep unions away from its door. The factory villages could be seen as a social contract of sorts between workers and the company; one in which both parties benefited. During hard times, such as the Great Depression, the company divided up the work so that every family and staff member received a salary they could survive on. The company also provided medical services for employees that became ill or injured, and even provided midwives when women gave birth.

The small villages were self-sufficient and consisted of houses for the workers, churches, schools, sports fields, shops of different kinds, and various common buildings. When the Cone Mills Corporation reached its zenith, two thousand six hundred seventy-five workers were living in approximately one thousand five hundred houses. East White Oak was a separate village for African-American employees who had the most unskilled jobs at the various factories.

In those times there came to be a nickname for the textile workers: "linthead". The workers, however, didn't take the insult lying down. If someone used this term in a derogatory way, he had to be prepared to get his teeth knocked out. The nickname came from the lint that constantly swirled around inside the factory and got stuck in the workers' hair. After a full day's work, their heads could be quite blue due to the indigo-colored dust cloud. For this reason, it wasn't difficult to recognize a Cone fabric worker.

Cone's denim is known for its high quality and durability. In 1915, Levi Strauss & Company became a customer and Cone has been producing denim for them ever since. Cone also had their own brand of denim called *Cone Deeptone Denim*, which they introduced to the work clothing market in 1936. Several of their customers used Deeptone, including Stonewall, Big Winston, Calf Skin, Big Red and J.C. Penney Super Big Mac. A tag reading Deeptone® Cone Denim was affixed to these other companies' branded clothing.

Deeptone was marketed for its durability, its strong and leathery "finish", and the promise it would maintain color longer. Marketing slogans such as "Deeptone: Insist on this label", or "Improve your 'overall appearance'" were used.

One might question why Cone did not use Deeptone denim to produce their own branded jeans?

The most likely answer is that they did not consider themselves experts in the manufacturing of pants themselves, and preferred to use their expertise in producing the fabric only. However, the widespread adoption of Deeptone denim by jean manufacturers affirms that Cone was a very strong and reputable company and therefore had the ability to negotiate – or even insist – on partnerships. Cone's excellent quality denim was, of course, a prerequisite for this.

Cone is one of the last companies in the United States that still produces *selvedge* denim. Selvedge – or *selfedge, selvege* – is a direct outcome of using old looms, which are narrower than the modern ones in use today. Unlike modern looms, the old looms leave the edges of the fabric unbroken, creating a sewn edge. The thread runs back and forth across the width of the fabric without it being cut off at the edges. The edge is called selvedge.

In old vintage jeans, different color selvedges were used, which identified the different styles of denim. Red, white, and yellow were common colors. Today's vintage selvedge styles use many colors which are more for fashion or accent.

The older looms made denim that was durable and suited for the workwear of that time. These days, larger modern looms make a wider denim fabric, which is less expensive to produce and much more efficient.

Selvedge denim began disappearing in the 1970s as companies replaced their old looms with new, wider ones. These looms also worked faster than the old ones, increased production and efficiencies and created a loom with fewer defects and imperfections than the vintage looms. But over time many felt that denim had lost a certain "personal character" associated with the earlier styles. But the cost efficiencies and speed of the newer looms still appealed to many jeans companies.

Recently, selvedge denim has come into vogue again as jean lovers want their garments to look like those from the good old days. For this reason, Cone Denim dusted off some of their old looms in the late 1990s, placed them back on the factory floor, and resumed production. It is also one of the reasons that White Oak Mills has survived financially. The renewed interest in selvedge has been a saving grace driven by today's fashion styles and the market's desire for all that is genuine and beautiful.

Viktor and Fredrik decide they will both use the images of Viktor's denim collection in their respective portfolios. Viktor's friend in the printing industry loves the photos and suggests that he contact a very driven woman who has started her own publishing house.

Viktor and his friend quickly arrange a meeting with Johanna, the CEO of the publishing house. They sit in her office in the center of town and talk over coffee. Viktor talks about what he does, about his collection and his great, historical denim puzzle. He pauses now and then to show Johanna the pictures that he and Fredrik have taken.

Johanna listens attentively and becomes infected by Viktor's enthusiasm. She proposes they make a book using all the fantastic material.

Viktor thinks about a combination of factors, but the one that feels most important to him is his mother's urging – she has been encouraging him to do something with his collection of jeans for a long time. Now, sitting there in the meeting, Viktor finally knows everything feels right about this opportunity. He has decided.

He thinks that it is time to put the pieces in place – so that not only he, but also anyone else who shares his passion for jeans – can see his beautiful puzzle.

INDIGOFERA TINCTORIA

CONE DEEPTONE

Pioneer was made by Deeptone Denim, one of Cone's highest quality fabrics. Cone collaborated with various jeans manufacturers, all of which used Deeptone Denim. For both Cone and the jeans companies, it was a way to ensure that the garments maintained high quality throughout production process, **making it a win-win situation for all involved.**

△ GREENSBORO, NORTH CAROLINA, 1941. Long lines of looms stretch out over the factory floor at the Cone Mills Corporation. When the mill is in full swing, blue lint gets whipped up into the air and sticks to the factory workers' hair and clothing. Most of them go home from work with blue tinted hair. This inspired outsiders to give them the nickname "lintheads". But after a while, Cone Mills employees came to wear it as a badge of honor.

△ THIS IS ONE OF CONE'S OLD LOOMS from the 1940s: an American Draper x3 fly shuttle loom. The fabrics produced on a loom like this are unique because they have irregularities and small errors that modern looms can't produce. Cone claims the reason for this is not only thanks to these old-fashioned machines. When the loom is in motion, it generates a particular rhythm in the old, cracking wooden floor which gets woven into the fabrics – and the personal character of the fabrics comes alive.

△ THIS PICTURE SHOWS detail of a pair of Pioneer Overalls from the 1930's.

△ PHOTOGRAPHER: Cory Piehowicz, *Bandit Photographer.*

△ VIKTOR'S FIRST ITEM to the collection.

THANKS

This book owes a great debt of gratitude to the many people who
have been involved in one way or another in its creation.

Michael Allen Harris and Charla Harris – without your help, this would have been
a much lesser book. Thank you for all the information and encouragement! The expertise
you have is unparalleled. You've served as the reference books we always needed.

Gratitude is further extended to Cory Piehowicz, who contributed the vintage photos found
in chapter two. Thank you, Cory! You've helped give the book an added dimension.

Brothers Douglas and Hampus Luhanko, as well as Oskar Eriksson, have been kind enough
to loan us the following denim garments which appear in the book: Pioneer, Pay Day overalls,
Gibraltar Triple Stitch shirt, Levi's rodeo club shirt, Levi's 705, and Lee 100J.
Many thanks to you!

In addition, others have contributed information, images, or simply lent
a hand during the project's completion. We would like to thank:
All the models.
Ingela and Anders from Marsfjäll Mountain Lodge.
Lars-Olof and Monica Svedberg.
Sandra Svensson och Markus Jonsson.
Debbie Behan Garrett, author and blogger.
Delores Sides at the International Textile Group, Inc.
Nancy White at H.D. Lee Company.
Tracey Panek at Levi Strauss & Company.
Nancy Larsson, proofreader.

We would also like to thank all the family members for allowing
their loved ones to participate in the project.

But above all, thanks to my parents – especially my mother, Maud Fredbäck
– who suggested I do something with my jeans collection.

VIKTOR FREDBÄCK